From Championship Wrestler to Road Rage Defendant

The Chris Harrison Story

Christopher T. Harrison

iUniverse, Inc.
Bloomington

From Championship Wrestler to Road Rage Defendant
The Chris Harrison Story

iUniverse books may be ordered through booksellers or by contacting:

iUniverse
1663 Liberty Drive
Bloomington, IN 47403
www.iuniverse.com
1-800-Authors (1-800-288-4677)

ISBN: 978-1-4620-6718-3 (sc)
ISBN: 978-1-4620-6719-0 (e)

Printed in the United States of America

iUniverse rev. date: 11/23/2011

Introduction

Although many great athletes have performed better at the championship level than me, few of them fortunately have become involved in *road rage*. See how I became an unwilling victim in 1984 and a defendant in 1997 under similar circumstances of *road rage*. Discover how an individual's faith enables one to persevere in life despite tremendous obstacles to one's path to success.

Acknowledgements

I wish to thank the Lord God Almighty and His Son and My Saviour, Jesus Christ, who have blessed me with a keen mind for remembering factual events and the foresight to maintain good notes during the many events of my life. This autobiography is particularly dedicated to the memory of my deceased mother Alma Janet Harrison and my deceased father Charles William Harrison. I would also like to honor the memory of my grandmothers Cecilia Fialkowski Lapka and Emily Richards Harrison as well as my grandfather William Bernard Harrison. I would specially like to dedicate this autobiography to the memory of my deceased wife Lavonia Faye Harrison, without whose love I would have never persevered in life. Finally I wish to thank my current wife Lena Lytton Harrison, for her patience with my difficult ways during our nearly seven years of marriage. Lena is truly my soul mate in love that I have sought and found.

CHAPTER 1

THE EARLY YEARS IN BALTIMORE

It was a bleak gray day in Baltimore, when Alma Janet Lapka married Charles William Harrison. It wasn't snowing and the Roman Catholic wedding went off without a hitch. The newlyweds did not take a honeymoon, but preferred to move into their new two bedroom and one bath bungalow in the suburbs of Baltimore named Dundalk. The neighbors dubbed the Harrisons as 'the honeymooners' from the big city.

Charles was twenty-two years young with curly, black hair and a chiseled, muscular body. He was a World War II naval veteran who purchased a new home with a fifty dollar down payment under the G.I. Bill of Rights. Of course a thirty year mortgage accompanied these new homes. Bill, as he preferred to be called(his middle name was William) took several jobs including selling insurance and working as a machinist to support his wife. He also played semi-pro football for Govans as an offensive guard at 170 pounds. Bill was a true competitor throughout his entire life. He also was an epileptic who consumed alcohol and had frequent seizures.

Alma, his bride, was a lithe, bespectacled twenty-two year old on a 5-foot 8-inch frame and black hair. She had worked for Hutzler's Department Store since her sixteenth birthday to help her mother with the financial responsibilities of their home. Both Alma and Bill had quit school in tenth grade. Both went to Patterson Park High School in east Baltimore and both came from working class families. Now they had each other and a working relationship.

Dundalk was a growing community in 1951. After World War II, the airport in Dundalk known as Logan Airfield, was subdivided into thousands of houses. Thus the term Logan Village came into existence. Alma and Bill owned one of these houses. All of these houses had matching roofs and shutters of black, green, red or yellow colors. Alma and Bill's house included the red variety. If you examine these houses today, none resembles the 1950s version of these houses. Due to Bill's efforts and other parents like him, many additions have accompanied these houses due to the influx of new children.

Dundalk was also in the midst of one of the great business complexes in the United States in the 1950s. Bethlehem Steel Plant at Sparrows Point Maryland, just two miles south of Dundalk, employed over 30,000 workers at one time. And just two miles north of Dundalk in Baltimore was a Chevrolet automotive plant which made large volumes of cars and trucks due to the steady train loads of steel. It was a perpetual cycle of blue collar workmanship that employed thousands of workers in the Baltimore metropolitan area. Dundalk lay in the epicenter of this vast conglomeration. Therefore the population grew quickly and pro-union sentiment sifted through Dundalk.

With all of these events occurring, I was born February 3, 1952, along with millions of other baby boomers that year. What an anniversary present for Alma and Bill Harrison! But the first child of their marriage was born and I was a cute, fat, bouncing baby boy at birth. Like most babies, I don't recall much about my infancy except that I was baptized a Catholic according to the baptismal certificate. By three years of age though, the memory button started to work. My mother said that I was the most hyperactive child that she had ever seen. Mom was actually ten pounds lighter when I was three years of age, than before she was pregnant. And she was thin when she got married. That same year I got my first spanking due to persistent wandering from an area. My parents and I had gone to Breezy Point Bathing Beach, which was adjacent to the Chesapeake Bay. After I entered the water, I sidestepped all of the adults, strolled across the beach, and disappeared into the wooded area beyond the beach. When I reappeared, after the lifeguards and my parents had fruitlessly combed the waters for a body, mom demanded that dad spank me. He grudgingly did so, but I had learned a lesson. This was not the last time that I learned a lesson the hard way. I was just a spoiled solitary son.

The next couple of years involved my mother teaching me everything about the English language. Her mother(my grandmother Lapka) was of Polish ancestry and raised my mother in an ethnically Polish section of Baltimore known as Canton. My mother attended Saint Casimir's School for eight years and was always grateful to the nuns there for their teaching of the English language to her. Mom truly excelled in her use of vocabulary.

By 1958 I was six years old and my life was about to experience major changes. I began first grade at Saint Rita's School, named after an Irish saint in an Irish-American community like Dundalk. Then on September 9th mom gave birth to my brother Robert. I was no longer the only child. But Robert had a major issue as he cried incessantly as an infant.

In the midst of all the sleepless nights at home, an event on December 28, 1958 revolutionized not only the sports world but placed the city of Baltimore on the sports map forever. The Baltimore Colts won the National Football League Championship game in 'sudden death overtime'. The repercussions of this event were enormous. By December 1958, many Americans had televisions and on that particular Sunday after Christmas over forty million fans tuned in to that particular game. What they saw was a riveting contest with David finally slaying Goliath. The unknown Baltimore Colts beat the favored stars from New York known as the Giants in New York 23 to 17. It was the first ever NFL Championship decided in overtime. The National Football League and Baltimore were never the same after that day. The success of the NFL spiraled beyond anyone's imagination due to the success of the "Greatest Game Ever Played". Baltimore fans, some 10,000 strong, welcomed the National Football League's latest champions at Friendship Airport that night. Alan Ameche, who scored the winning touchdown in overtime, was the guest star on *The Ed Sullivan Show* that evening. In 1958, *The Ed Sullivan Show* was the most popular entertainment show in America. It remained that way until 1971. In 1959, the Baltimore Colts repeated as NFL Champions when they vanquished the same New York Giants in Baltimore. We were number one in America, at least in the National Football League.

By December 1959 the Harrison family had another addition with the birth of my sister Janet on December 26th. I do not believe that there was ever a happier baby that has been born. She slept constantly and when she awakened, she played and then she ate or drank her formula. After that brief interlude, she returned to sleep. As the 1960s began, my dad was laid off from work for nearly six months and our family had reached five members. Needless to say, my family's financial outlook was bleak. But events in the world and our community changed our plight.

My father applied for a position with the Baltimore City Police Department. Dad had top-notch arithmetic skills and with his physical abilities, I thought that he could become the perfect cop. But dad had epilepsy and failed the physical examination due to this condition. It was the first and the last time that I ever saw my dad cry. It was the only position that he aspired to be in life. As a result my parents borrowed money from dad's parents to keep our home. But my mother was adamant about my enrollment in Catholic school. Family financial failures did not compel my parents to enroll me in public school, when I was a good student in a parochial one.

When John F. Kennedy became the new president of the United States, it turned into a godsend for our family. Dad had passed the postal clerical examination in 1960 and had not received any information about a position there. When Kennedy started his presidency, the post office began a new hiring campaign. Dad started his new position as a part-time clerk in August of 1961, working many hours initially. As time passed into years, our family began to benefit financially. Dad remained a postal clerk until his retirement in August 1987. The Post Office unlike the Baltimore City Police Department did not discriminate against a World War II naval veteran with an honorable discharge even if he had epilepsy.

By 1962 my mother gave birth to her last child. My brother

Michael was born Friday the 13th in July of that year. He seemed like a normal baby, crying occasionally and sleeping the rest of the time. Mom said that he was her last child and she was right. Now there were six of us and dad constantly added bedrooms to an unfinished attic to accompany our sleeping needs. But mom kept the six of us in line.

In February 1964, I watched something on television that had a huge impact on my life. The Maryland Scholastic Association (MSA) Wrestling championship finals were on television showcasing the 154 pound weight class. The MSA was composed of over twenty private and public schools in the greater Baltimore area. The black entrant from Baltimore City College High School was undefeated with six straight pins during the season. A pin is when you hold your opponent's shoulders to the mat for one second, thus ending the match before six minutes has elapsed, which is the normal ending period of a wrestling match. In this particular match, his opponent, a white wrestler from Loyola High School decisively defeated the Baltimore City College wrestler by decision for the MSA championship. The black entrant from City College was a middleweight version of Hercules and still lost the match, despite his muscular physique. My goal from that day forward was to wrestle for a championship some day.

At that time period, I was in sixth grade, about a hundred pounds soaking wet, and Saint Rita's School had no wrestling programs. But there were scuffles on the playground and I was involved in my fair share of these. I played Little League baseball for Saint Rita's, but I was a poor baseball player, who could not hit nor catch. But I did play YMCA football that year. I played aged nine to twelve football at twelve years of age, but didn't start until the last game of the year against rival Sparrows Point YMCA. Dundalk and I were hopelessly outclassed in the Steel Bowl. At this juncture, I was a pathetic excuse for an athlete.

By 1966 I was in eighth grade and decisions about my future were made in that year. I either attended public school in Dundalk, which was co-educational, or a new parochial all-boys high school in the city. My hormones were raging, but I didn't have a clue at fourteen years of age about the birds and bees and specifically sex. Being the oldest child had its drawbacks as there were no older siblings to fill in the sordid details about the opposite sex. I did have a 'crush' on a female classmate at Saint Rita's School, but she made it quite clear, that she wasn't the least bit interested in me. As a matter of fact, none of my classmates liked me. I attended the eighth grade graduation party without an invitation. It was there that I was snubbed by my former classmates from Saint Rita's School.

In March 1966, I attended orientation for incoming ninth graders at Archbishop Curley High School. The school, which was only five years old, was preparing for its second graduation. My Saint Rita's classmates and I attended on a Saturday. With tuition at two hundred dollars a year and my brother Robert and sister Janet enrolled at Saint Rita's School, the cost of tuition was steep for my family. But dad worked steadily for the post office and mom worked for the US Army at Fort Holabird as a file clerk. My family was more financially viable than ever. Even I worked as a newspaper carrier, earning six dollars per week in 1966. Dad insisted that I pay him one dollar a week in return for room and board in preparation for the financial responsibilities of adult life.

The summer of 1966 produced a sequence of events that propelled me to attend Archbishop Curley in the fall with a renewed sense of purpose. Most of the high school students in my neighborhood were older than me and some of them bullied me. During that summer my neighbor pushed me into a car after a little scuffle between the two of us. The push created a sizeable dent on a vehicle at the Logan Village Shopping Center. As there was a two hundred dollar reward on the vehicle's visor for any information pertaining to damage to that vehicle, the local kids informed the police about my solitary role in the incident. The police arrived at my parent's house and informed them about my part in damaging that vehicle. Of course, only my name arose during the conversation. While this conversation occurred, I listened to the lies in the bathtub. After the police and the liars left, I emerged from the bathroom and told my parents the truth about the incident in question. I was at fault, but I wasn't the only one responsible for the damage in this case. But the story had a happy ending. My neighbor, who was involved in the incident, told my parents the truth and offered to pay half of the damage to the vehicle. Well at least I had one true friend in Dundalk.

At times I was my own worst enemy. That summer, Merritt Point Beach in Dundalk was closed due to the pollution caused by Bethlehem Steel. The beach on the Patapsco River, which was the main tributary between Baltimore and the Chesapeake Bay, had been opened during the previous year. I was determined and foolhardy to swim in the water and the pollution in its depths nearly caused me to lose my hearing. By August, I spent a lot of time in the bedroom with persistent earaches and constant pain. Mom, in her maternal wisdom, decided that I needed a doctor. The resident ear surgeon in Dundalk saved my hearing. But that wasn't my only pathetic character defect at that time.

I started smoking cigarettes at thirteen years of age and dad was disappointed in this behavior. But dad said as long as I smoked only in the living room and paid for this bad habit, I was allowed to do so. If I faltered in this matter, all smoking privileges were revoked. That is what I loved about my parents, as they gave you conditions and you had a responsibility to uphold them. If you failed, you had only yourself to blame. Nevertheless, I needed change in my pathetic life and Archbishop Curley High School was the perfect place where I found it. It was one of the best decisions of my life, as it saved me from foolishness.

CHAPTER 11

ATTENDING A BALTIMORE CITY HIGH SCHOOL IN THE RIOTOUS 1960S

Archbishop Curley High School was a three story structure of assorted classrooms and laboratories with an auditorium, gymnasium and cafeteria annex. Additionally the Friary, where the priests resided, adjoined the auditorium and the chapel. This conglomerate lie on the northwest sector of approximately thirty-five acres of land in east Baltimore where Erdman Avenue and Sinclair Lane intersect. On those acres of land was a football field enclosed by a bowl, a baseball field, soccer field, football practice area and a faculty/student parking lot. The school was administered by the Franciscan Friars, an order dedicated to the memory of Saint Francis of Assisi. They wore black robes with a white cord around their waist. Hence the school's nickname was the Friars, the school yearbook was called the Cord, and the school's colors were black and white. The friars and the lay teachers that the school employed, were as dedicated a group of teachers as I have ever known. The school was named after the former archbishop of Baltimore who oversaw the diocese from the 1920s to the 1940s. The school was subsidized by the Archdiocese of Baltimore, meaning that it was cheaper to attend Archbishop Curley than some of the more traditional parochial schools. In 1966 Mount Saint Joseph charged four hundred dollars a year tuition, while Loyola and Calvert Hall both charged eight hundred dollars tuition per year. So Curley was truly a bargain at two hundred dollars tuition per year with the dedicated professionals that we had teaching us all the skills that were necessary. My freshmen class consisted of over three hundred and fifty applicants. After screen testing, less than three hundred of these applicants became students. By 1966 Curley had about one thousand students between the classes of 1967 through 1970 inclusive.

We began the school year after Labor Day with a Mass, which was the Catholic way of enlisting God's help for all of the students during the new academic year. Then it was off to our respective homerooms and special interests. As I stated earlier, football had been king in Baltimore since at least 1958, with the emergence of the Colts as the National Football League champions. But my new high school, the Curley Friars had quite a powerhouse football team in the fall of 1966. The previous two varsity football seasons had produced just one win and one tie against our rival Cardinal Gibbons, whose school had just been constructed in 1962. But this football team's spectacular debut was a solid thrashing of John Carroll School. The following week dad and I went to Patterson and watched Curley defeat dad's old school. I fell in love with football at that point and determined to try out for the Curley football team the following year. Football was my first love, while wrestling was put on the back burner. Curley crushed Dunbar and Southern easily in successive weeks. We had a good football team because we had a senior quarterback and wide receiver who combined for eight touchdowns in the first four games. Additionally we had a sensational sophomore running back, who at six foot tall and two hundred pounds, had several touchdowns and many yards rushing. Finally one of our senior linemen was selected as the Maryland Scholastic Association's Unsung Hero of 1966. By this time Curley had almost as much sports coverage in the *Baltimore Sunpapers* as the Baltimore Orioles, who swept the Los Angeles Dodgers and Sandy Koufax in the World Series in October of that year.

However in the fifth game of the football season, Curley's bubble burst. Undefeated Curley traveled to McDonogh School, whom had just one loss for the season. McDonogh had barely won each of their four games by the slimmest of margins. On the first series of downs, Curley received the ball and advanced the ball rapidly to the McDonogh five yard line in just a handful of plays. On first and goal to goal, our senior quarterback threw to his favorite receiver in the end zone, but the football was intercepted. The McDonogh defensive back ran 103 yards for a touchdown. The Curley Friars amassed over three hundred offensive yards compared to McDonogh's twenty-five yards for the game, but still lost by six points. Now Curley knew how the other four teams felt that had lost to McDonogh, if that was any kind of consolation.

While the football team fared well, I did well in academics. I made second honors on the first report card and remained on the honor roll during freshman year. At least I was a perfect fit for high school in the academic sense. Athletically I was an abysmal failure at five foot six inches tall and one hundred thirty pounds without muscle tone and a smoking habit. But

I experienced a lot of change that year. In physical education class, the ninth graders ran a half mile course. I was the next to last runner, when an obese two hundred pound freshman passed me down the stretch. I was out of breath and panting. I knew this was due to smoking but the new classmates did not care. They mocked me for stopping and chastised me for being out of shape. I quit smoking the following week forever.

Meanwhile Curley's football team stumbled down the stretch. After the McDonogh debacle, Curley lost to Gilman and Forest Park in successive weeks. The Friars were eliminated from the 'B' Conference championship. The following week Curley pummeled Carver High and secured their first winning season ever in varsity football. But there remained one more regular season game against our rival Cardinal Gibbons. In front of approximately one thousand cold fans, the Cardinal Gibbons Crusaders defeated the home team Archbishop Curley Friars. It was a great game to watch and an inspiring season for the students, who all felt like winners.

Football season ended but it inspired one to play football and wrestle that much more. I knew that I needed to improve my physique, so I started regular workouts at home with pushups and sit ups. My breathing improved due to the cessation of smoking and I was prepared to be an athlete, even jogging in the street for a short distance. I was determined to become a good athlete and wished to remain a good student.

By August of 1967, I weighed one hundred sixty pounds, ran the hundred yard dash in fifteen seconds, and did a repetition of fifty pushups. These were hardly earth shattering facts, but progress was made in six months of physical conditioning. Varsity football practice started and I thought that a year experience of YMCA football would help me to make the varsity football team. I was in for a rude awakening as all of Curley's athletes on the practice field were better football players. Football requires a lot of quick reactions to situations on the field and my knowledge of offensive schemes was sadly deficient. For my efforts, I was relegated to the JV football team as a third string player. Curley's JV football team had a terrible record that year, so all of us needed improvement. The varsity was almost as woeful with a losing record for the football season too. Part of the varsity's losing record was due to the departure of Curley's three senior stars and their classmates from the previous year. The other reason our varsity football team plummeted, was due to the injury of our star junior running back, who missed most of the season.

The only bright spot for Curley during the fall of 1967 was the soccer team. They won all year to advance to the MSA championship game and faced perennial power Patterson. Curley got thumped in the soccer championship at Kirk Field. Patterson's soccer team won many MSA soccer championships in the 1960s and in 1967 Curley became its latest conquest. Nevertheless Archbishop Curley experienced its first championship game.

During that particular year the sophomore jinx hit me hard in the academic arena. I barely passed my courses and had to be disciplined by some of my teachers due to lack of self control. I loved Curley but had a tough time coping with authority then.

Nevertheless I tried out for the wrestling team. I practiced but didn't wrestle in any of the matches. I don't even remember the name of the wrestling coach. The only bright spot for our varsity wrestling team was that we had a senior heavyweight, who won many matches and reached the quarterfinals of the MSA Wrestling Tournament, but lost on a referee's decision. A referee's decision occurs when two mat judges and a referee decide in their opinion which wrestler deserves to win the match after the match is tied after overtime. Curley's senior star heavyweight played center on the varsity football team and after graduation, participated in sports for the University of Maryland.

The most significant event of my sophomore year took place in April 1968 when Doctor Martin Luther King Jr. was assassinated by a white man in Memphis, Tennessee. The TET offensive in Vietnam in January 1968 was tumultuous too, but it paled in comparison to the racial turmoil that we experienced in Baltimore. King's assassination in April was literally lighting the torch to the dynamite. From our vantage point in Dundalk, we saw the flames of fire from west Baltimore high in the sky over the Patapsco River that dark Saturday night. On Easter Sunday, Governor Agnew ordered a dusk-to-dawn curfew with the National Guard patrolling the streets of Baltimore. There were even more fires the following night in the streets. Baltimore was in the midst of a traumatic racial war.

I went to school the following Tuesday, hoping that tempers had subsided. But I was dead wrong in my optimistic outlook. Most of the students at Curley at that time used the metropolitan buses to reach school and return home. Normally I walked a half mile to Girls' Catholic High School on Edison Avenue and caught a #22 bus to Highlandtown, an ethnically white neighborhood in east Baltimore. From there I transferred to the #10 bus, which traveled to Dundalk.

On this particular day, I and two friends boarded the #22 bus. Each of us wore a sports coat, tie and trousers, which was Curley's dress code. The bus driver was black and all of the other students with the exception of us, were also black. The bus driver cautioned us to remain near him at the front, and prepare to exit after he stopped the bus. He drove the bus over a mile on Edison Highway while the large group of black students on the bus, inched closer to the three white students. Suddenly the bus driver hit the brake and told us to run for our lives. We galloped about a half mile to the Chevrolet dealership at Monument Street near Highland Avenue. In 1968 that was the boundary of an ethnically white neighborhood. We were finally safe from harm. The three of us owe our lives to that bus driver. He was truly an unsung hero in a racially violent time in Baltimore.

In my junior year at Curley, I tried out for the football team again as a defensive lineman. I had absorbed some knowledge of football from the previous year's participation and was a chiseled one hundred sixty pounds at five foot eight inches tall. I played reasonably well in preseason and was one of the last four athletes cut from the varsity football team that year. For a lot of reasons I decided not to play JV football during that particular fall. However, all of our football teams including varsity, junior varsity, and freshmen-sophomore played extremely well. The varsity, in particular, excelled in every game. In the opener, Curley crushed Woodlawn, a Baltimore County powerhouse. Woodlawn actually won the Baltimore County football championship that same season. But Curley was in the 'B' Conference of the Maryland Scholastic Association, which was a much stronger division. Our rivalry with Cardinal Gibbons was a disappointment as the Friars suffered a one point loss at home. But Cardinal Gibbons was in the 'A' Conference of the MSA and therefore the game was inconsequential officially. The third game of the season was the first game of Curley's 'B' Conference schedule. In those days in the Maryland Scholastic Association, the 'A' Conference was like playing AAA schools in the state, the 'B' Conference was like playing AA schools in the state, and the 'C' Conference was like playing A schools at the state level.

Curley then went into maximum overdrive in the 'B' Conference, crushing Carver, Dunbar, and Southern in successive weeks. Just like two years earlier, Curley faced McDonogh again. Both were undefeated in the conference, but this one had a different result. McDonogh took a twenty point lead into the fourth quarter at home. Curley then scored three straight touchdowns in the fourth quarter to tie the score and the game. The following week Curley defeated Gilman in one of the most explosive offensive shootouts in MSA high school football history. Curley was still undefeated in the 'B' Conference with its last two games at home against Forest Park and Patterson. Forest Park was also undefeated in the conference and with the 'B' Conference championship on the line, they defeated Curley by two points. Their great running back had one more rushing yard than our great senior running back and Forest Park won by the slimmest of margins. Our guys were heart-broken. The last game of the season produced a demolition of rival Patterson for a second place finish in the conference. We were three points from an undefeated season and finished with six wins, two losses and a tie.

However, Curley tasted its first varsity championship during the fall of 1968. The soccer team defeated powerful Patterson at Kirk Field by a single goal with three minutes left in the game. At last the student body erupted with a message "We're Number 1" and meant every word of it. It was not the last time that this phrase was used at Curley during that particular school year.

Meanwhile wrestling season began in November and I was determined to impress our new coach. Curley couldn't have recruited a better coach. He was a stocky, short man with an eye defect. When he spoke, he always gave one a sideward glance. But our wrestling coach taught us wrestling techniques and conditioned our bodies well. I discovered a lot of wrestling moves from our new coach. Being on a learning roll in wrestling, I also got on an academic roll and earned second honors during the first quarter of the school year. As the wrestling season started, I was the varsity 154 pound starter through a wrestle-off. But as a result of that wrestle-off, I hyper extended my elbow and did not wrestle in the opener against Saint Paul's School. I was in a lot of pain and was relegated to junior varsity during the following week. Our junior varsity and I won our first match of the season against Southern High School. After the Christmas holidays ended, the junior varsity and I got our second straight victory against Northwestern. But I wanted to wrestle varsity though I could not defeat our winless 154 pound wrestler in a wrestle-off. A wrestle-off is where a varsity starter is challenged by a junior varsity wrestler for his position. If the junior varsity wrestler wins the match, he assumes the varsity position. If he loses or even ties the varsity starter, that starter maintains his position during that week. I believe it is the fairest way in sports to determine a starter at any level. But I lost the wrestle-off and remained at the junior varsity level.

In the midst of this on January 12, 1969 the entire sports

world was shocked by a development in the Super Bowl. The New York Jets, who were 17 point Super Bowl underdogs, defeated our favored Baltimore Colts by nine points in the big game. It was a development that gave hope to underdogs everywhere. I was certainly an underdog at that time. On Tuesday of that week our junior varsity ventured to Patterson and won our match, while our varsity dropped a close match at home to Patterson. Our varsity 175 pound wrestler injured himself badly and ended his season. With the position available, I and a senior 154 pound grappler wrestled for the position. I won the wrestle-off and started the following match against Loyola at the varsity level. Curley's varsity wrestling team had produced a mediocre record and needed a win badly against our Catholic rivals, whom had never lost to us.

I had actually starved myself to reach 141 pounds that Tuesday against Patterson in my third straight junior varsity win. But in preparation for Friday's match, I ate two suppers and gained enough weight to wrestle at the 175 pound weight class. I reached 147 pounds before the match, so I was only thirty pounds underweight. Fortunately our light weights did a fantastic job against Loyola and we held an eight point advantage by the onset of my match. With five points awarded to a team for a pin and three points awarded to a team for a decision, Loyola needed two pins to win the match. As there were only two matches left and we had a good heavyweight, that was highly unlikely. But a pin against me was essential for Loyola to tie the match. That's when our coach told me "Just give me six." Our coach wanted me to finish the six minute match and not to get pinned. As the match progressed, I had other ideas.

In an individual wrestling match points are awarded

in several ways. When the match begins both wrestlers are standing freely or in a neutral position. If one wrestler takes down the other wrestler, he is awarded two points for controlling his opponent. This is the first period of a match and lasts two minutes. The second period of the match is also of two minute duration but with both wrestlers in a referees' position, where one wrestler is on his hands and knees and the other is atop of him. The positions of the wrestlers are then reversed in the third and final two minute period. If a wrestler escapes control from the bottom position he receives one point and if he reverses his position, gaining control of the initial top opponent, he receives two points for a reversal. The goal is always to pin your opponent and end the match as quickly as possible. But you can receive two points for a predicament when your opponent's shoulders are turned at a ninety degree angle to the mat or three points for a near fall, when you nearly pin your opponent, but can't flatten his shoulders for one second. One point for riding time is awarded when you control your opponent for one minute more than he controls you during the match. You can also score two points this way if you control your opponent two minutes more than he controls you during the length of the match.

As for my Loyola opponent at the 175 pound weight class, he had previously pinned his opponent from Southern High. So he was a good varsity wrestler and barely made weight. But our match became a dogfight and at the end, a nightmare for Loyola High School. With seventeen seconds left, I held the top referees' position in a tie. He nearly escaped to get one point for the win, but I held his foot and ankle and kept that from happening at the time. The match ended and I was awarded one point for riding time to win my first varsity decision. Curley had clinched the win and the heavyweight match was inconsequential. Actually both heavyweights tied as Curley secured the win. My teammates gave me a ride on their shoulders around the Loyola gymnasium and I was named the 'Curley Wrestler of the Week'. I was also nominated for the *Baltimore Sunpapers* high school athlete of the week, but was outvoted by a 5-foot 4-inch tall guard from Dunbar who scored forty-six points in a big basketball game against rival City College High School. What a week for underdogs in Baltimore!

As for Dunbar, they became the next wrestling victim of the Curley Friars. I suffered my first mat loss by decision at 165 pounds, but our varsity improved to four wins and two losses for the season. The following week Forest Park ventured to Curley for a big match. We wrestled them in the cafeteria as the basketball team used the gymnasium for a home game. But wrestling in the cafeteria was nothing new to us as the team moved chairs and tables on a daily basis there, in preparation for wrestling practice. But in January 1969 we lost to Forest Park there. I lost to an undefeated wrestler by decision who was the MSA Wrestling Tournament's 165 pound finalist in February. I lasted the entire match with Forest Park's version of Hercules, who pinned all of his previous opponents. Although I was satisfied with my effort, I was disappointed that our team's record fell. That disappointment paled when compared with the following week's match. We were embarrassed by Mergenthaler Vocational Technical High School at home. I got pinned in twenty-four seconds at the 165 pound weight class. The varsity wrestling team lost again with one match left in the season. However, the junior varsity wrestling team continued its undefeated season with a victory over Mergenthaler at their facility.

Curley's last varsity match was against Northern High at home and we won easily. Our varsity wrestling team finished with a winning record and the junior varsity defeated Northern and won the 'B' Conference championship with an undefeated record. We were number one again. Curley's JV wrestling team joined the JV soccer team with championship trophies attained during that year. Although I was satisfied in aiding the junior varsity in their success, I was disappointed in my varsity record. I missed the Northern match and lost weight to reach the 141 pound weight class for the upcoming MSA Wrestling Tournament.

Curley's wrestling team as a group in 1969 was a mixture of question marks and qualified talent. Several of my teammates including me were in the former category. The latter category consisted of our two co-captains, of whom one was unbeaten at the 120 pound weight class and the other had just one loss at 145 pounds. Our junior 165 pound entrant and our senior heavyweight also had winning records and were seeded in their respective weight classes. So it wasn't shocking for Curley to fare well in the MSA Wrestling Tournament. Actually our 120 pound entrant wrestled extremely well, and became the first Curley wrestler to win the MSA Wrestling Tournament in his weight class! Our other co-captain won his initial match and then lost his second match in the round of sixteen and was eliminated from the tournament. He experienced mononucleosis and remained sick, spending several days in the hospital. Our senior heavyweight picked up the slack and finished fifth in the tournament. The rest of the team was basically one and done except one.

Every tournament has a story and our 154 pound entrant became the story of the 1969 wrestling tournament. This senior was winless all year prior to the tournament. He lost his initial match to the top seed in his weight class from City College by a one point decision. All of his teammates including me, thought the top seed was overrated or our guy just caught him on a bad day. Those ideas were far from the truth. The top seed pinned his way to the championship finals and won that match easily by points. Our guy won his first match of the season in a consolation match on Friday afternoon after the quarterfinals. An hour later he won his second match immediately before the semi-finals. That night he won his third consolation match of the day and was assured of at least a sixth pace finish in his weight class, which consisted of twenty-three wrestlers. On Saturday before the championship finals, he won his fourth straight decision in one day. Now he wrestled for third place in his weight class. Our wrestler took a four point lead into the final period of the match against a Gilman wrestler whom had just one loss. But with thirty seconds left in the match, his adversary slammed our wrestler onto his back and pinned him with five seconds left. Had our wrestler survived the slam, he would have won the match by a point. But a fourth place finish at the 154 pound weight class in the MSA Wrestling Tournament was truly a remarkable feat for our senior entrant who was winless all year.

The rest of Curley's wrestling team was one and done including me. But I did learn a vital lesson. Preparing for my match in the round of sixteen against an eighth-seeded opponent from Carver, I quipped to my coach, that a tough match loomed for me the following day against the top seed. My coach told me "Worry about today or there won't be a tomorrow for you." He was right as I lost by decision and was eliminated from the tournament. The opponent from Carver finished fourth in that weight class and the top seed from City College won it. Curley finished in seventh place out of twenty-three schools with a total of twenty-six points. I finished the season with a four win and four loss record in my initial season of wrestling. But I loved the sport and desired to improve my game in the worst way by the following year.

If the cry "We're Number One" sounded redundant by now, you needed to avoid Curley's spring sports season of 1969. Beginning with our 'A' Conference baseball powerhouse through our talented 'B' Conference lacrosse team to our multi-dimensional track and field team, Archbishop Curley became the championship school of the MSA. Our varsity baseball team won their initial 'A' Conference championship by defeating arch rival Cardinal Gibbons in a two out of three game series. Curley won the first game at home, Gibbons won by one run at their facility and Curley won the deciding game at Memorial Stadium. Our JV baseball team also won their initial 'A' Conference championship by defeating Loyola in a two out of three series as well. Curley's varsity lacrosse team won their initial 'B' Conference championship by defeating John Carroll in the final game. Finally our track and field team broke several individual MSA records on their way to the best finish in school history. Our team came in second place in the 'A' Conference to perennial power City College High School. City College won every track and field meet from 1957 to 1972. So it was a great accomplishment to finish second to them in track and field in the 'A' Conference. In eight short years Archbishop Curley High School had become a model of excellence in athletics as well as academics.

With all of the success that my high school had experienced, I looked forward to senior year. Actually I was a good student, ranked twenty-eighth out of two hundred seventy-eight in the junior class. I wanted to attend college, but did not know where to go. By May 1969 I started a busboy job at the Brentwood Inn, a posh restaurant on the Baltimore City line and two miles from home. My days of newspaper delivery ended and life changed drastically over the next twelve months. The Brentwood Inn and I became well acquainted over the next several years.

THE WILD SUMMER OF 1969 AND MY SENIOR YEAR

The summer of 1969 was probably the most turbulent summer in the history of the United States. The 1960s, which had seen a lot of political and social upheaval, experienced major turbulence that summer. On July 20, 1969, our astronauts landed on the moon and collected soil samples, while many viewed this event on television. In August, Charles Manson and his followers went on a rampage in California, and murdered several people. Also in August, a solitary rural town called Woodstock New York observed some of the loudest rock and roll music and raunchiest sexual escapades ever viewed by the camera. In addition to everything else, there was a hurricane named Camille, which took the lives of many people. It caused numerous deaths in a town named Buena Vista Virginia and left waves of destruction by flooding in Baltimore. Dundalk was under three feet of water at that time.

During that summer I took a driver's education course at Patterson High. I met some of their female students and liked the scenery. The opposite sex at Patterson was definitely appealing to me. I also liked the waitresses at the Brentwood Inn, most of whom were in their twenties. My hormones were raging and I didn't have a clue as to what to do about it. I was seventeen years old with copper skin and black hair on a 5-foot 8-inch frame and 175 pounds of weight. My body contained bulging biceps, chest, and shoulders atop a thirty-one inch waist. But with my educational knowledge, I didn't have a clue about sex. Without any older siblings to coach me, I relied on *Playboy magazine* for knowledge of the opposite sex. I worked out like crazy, sometimes doing eight hundred to a thousand repetitions of pushups daily when the Brentwood Inn didn't schedule me to work. On days that I worked it was only two to three hundred repetitions of pushups. Although I had a good physique, I didn't know what to do with it then.

My dad had an idea of what to do with it and arranged for me to receive a letter of introduction to the US Naval Academy from an old boyhood pal who had become a circuit court judge. Dad was pro-Vietnam and since he was an enlisted man in the US Navy, he wanted his oldest son to be an officer in the US Navy. For my part, I barely passed the US Naval Academy screening test and went there in July for orientation. After I asked about the availability of females, I was told that the Naval Academy had no females and probably would never have any females at that institution. Furthermore upon graduation, the US Navy required one's services for an additional five years. I was distraught and spoke to a naval captain there about my dilemma and he curtailed my candidacy for the US Naval Academy. My thinking at the time was that I wouldn't be able to consort with females until I was twenty-seven years of age and that was too long of a time period without a woman.

After all there was still one more year of attendance at all-boy Archbishop Curley High School.

My dad was furious with me about how I had embarrassed the family and him in front of his judge friend. I did not want to attend the US Naval Academy at that time. I salute those who serve our country and later in life, I served my country honorably in the US Army. But I wasn't ready at seventeen years of age for a lot of reasons. Dad lamented about how it was impossible for me to attend college without a scholarship, when he had three other school age children at home. What I regretted the most is that from that day forward, there was a rift between dad and me until his death in 2003.

That summer the family had an Ocean City vacation. Ocean City is an eight mile stretch of motels, restaurants, and arcades on the eastern shore of Maryland adjacent to the Atlantic Ocean. Naturally Ocean City has much in the way of swimming, fishing, and boating. Although I lost dad's fishing rod in the Pocomoke River, the family still had a good time. Nevertheless, dad lamented for years about his lost fishing rod. Dad helped me in another matter that summer though. After I had successfully passed the driver's education course at Patterson, I asked him for his advice about a possible driver's license. His answer was simple. If one bought a car and drove it, one had to make car payments, pay for automobile insurance and gasoline. In order to do that, one needed a daily job, not just two nights a week. But if I continued my current job schedule, I had enough money to ride the buses and continue my academic and athletic pursuits. As dad said, a driver's license could be attained after high school graduation. I had a senior year left and wanted to live it to the fullest, without additional financial responsibilities.

Football practice started in the middle of August amid tremendous heat and humidity. A week later Hurricane Camille caused massive flooding in Baltimore specifically in Dundalk. The water was three feet deep and rose to the height of the first floor of our home. Rowboats and canoes dotted the landscape of Loganview Drive. Fortunately the water receded quickly and I returned to football practice. We practiced hard, with two-a-day sessions, the law of the land at Archbishop Curley High School. This was senior year and I was determined to become a member of the varsity football team. I began practice as a second string varsity guard and soon regressed to third string on the depth chart, due to ignorance of football offensive and defensive schemes. I was self-destructing again, but ran an 11.9 second time in the hundred yard dash. It was my fastest one hundred yard dash ever and I was physically stronger. Where this path took me was beyond my wildest imagination.

Curley was picked to finish in seventh place out of eight schools in the 'B' Conference that year by a committee of football coaches. That fact was never lost on our two varsity football coaches. They chided us daily about respect. But by the end of football season, we earned everyone's respect. In our first preseason scrimmage we played Mount Saint Joseph, another Catholic all-boys school from west Baltimore. They were the *Baltimore Sunpapers'* preseason pick to be #1 in the Maryland Scholastic Association. Surprisingly Curley won the scrimmage on a fluke play. Our coach was unhappy that we were outplayed, but I sure liked being on the winning side of one of those games. We also won our second scrimmage against favored Lancaster Catholic in Lancaster Pennsylvania by a single touchdown. But I played poorly, as I got knocked backward to the ground by a tackling dummy while practicing and then lost a fumble that squirted from under my body during the scrimmage. At this juncture, I didn't even know if I would make the varsity football team as the season started, but the coaches kept seniors on the varsity and played them if possible.

By the beginning of September 1969, there was a number one song on the pop charts called *Bridge Over Troubled Waters* by Simon and Garfunkel. Some thought the song referred to the Vietnam War, some thought it referred to racial unrest in places like Baltimore, but some of the football team thought it referred to us. Nevertheless the song had been #1 since football practice started in mid-August, and remained #1 until the second week of November. Not even the greatest musical hits by the Beatles eclipsed that thirteen week duration as the number one hit on the pop charts. Some on the football team thought the song would carry us to victory all year. In our last preseason scrimmage we tied Saint Paul's Episcopalian School. The football scoring theme was therefore set. We had difficulty scoring but were unscored upon during the scrimmages. This was a gritty bunch who struggled to win most of their games.

School started with a Catholic Mass after Labor Day and senior year officially began. I especially looked forward to this September as I was a member of the varsity football team, although relegated to the bench. Our team had nine games that year, five of which occurred in October. All three of our home games took place that month meaning that our remaining six games were on the road. Our first game in September was against Woodlawn, the defending Baltimore County champions at their stadium,. We scored twenty points in the first quarter and looked great. But our scoring stopped and they scored a touchdown and an extra two point conversion in the fourth quarter. Woodlawn moved the ball well again, but we stopped them on downs. Coach was upset with our performance, and told us to improve before the next game against Cardinal Gibbons or "they will hand your helmets to you." But we ignored his warnings, as we won our first game of the season and did not lose any scrimmages. Cardinal Gibbons was winless, having lost to Georgetown Prep, the #2 football team in America, and Dematha, a perennial powerhouse. Coach said Cardinal Gibbons was the best winless team in the country, but we weren't the least bit concerned about that.

That Saturday was a beautiful day about eighty degrees, when we started playing Gibbons at their stadium. Gibbons scored on the opening kickoff and led Curley by twelve points before halftime. We had the ball close to their goal line prior to halftime, but squandered an opportunity to get back into the game. In the third quarter, Cardinal Gibbons scored two more touchdowns and put the game out of reach. Gibbons won easily by four touchdowns. I was ejected in the fourth quarter, for a block in the back and a subsequent punch in the mouth. Even then my temper got me into trouble. Our coach said that I would never play for him again. But I was one of many Curley players that were ejected from that game for fighting. The boys in black and white had a lot to learn and not just about football. At the same time Patterson annihilated Mount Saint Joseph, whom Curley had barely survived in our first scrimmage. The road was getting rougher by the minute.

Our Monday practice after the debacle was the longest single one that I ever experienced in football. We stayed on the field late and in the classroom later. Our coach decided on a six man line and two linebacker defense for the rest of the football season. In addition to those eight defensive players we had three backs in our basic defensive scheme. The two linebackers covered a lot of territory and were the backbone of the defense. We had two players who were over six feet tall and two hundred pounds in weight. Both were smart, savvy football players with great speed. The one player ran the one hundred yard dash in 10.9 seconds, which was sprinters' speed. The other player was slower, but had the raw power to break a blocking sled. With our two best athletes running the defense, our football season was saved.

Our first home game of the season was the first Friday in October and that opponent was Carver High, a vocational public school from west Baltimore. In three years of high school, Curley had basically beaten Carver in football and this game was similar. Curley led by three touchdowns when I entered the game on defense in the fourth quarter. Carver was on their own three yard line and our second string defense yearned for a safety, which is two points on the scoreboard for tackling the opposition in their own end zone. Our defensive tackle then popped the football loose from their running back and I was suddenly in position to scoop up the football and score a touchdown. Instead my best friend yelled "Chris block!" and I whirled to see him and a Carver player near me. I reacted by throwing a perfect body block into my Carver foe and my buddy scored the fourth Curley touchdown of the game. I joked with him about depriving one of a moment of glory and hoped that the *Baltimore Sunpapers* would misspell his name the following day, which they did. However, it was satisfying to block for a touchdown, when one had never done it before. Curley scored four touchdowns in four quarters without a single extra point. In a close game that could haunt you. We had won our first conference game of the season.

The following game was against Dunbar, an inner city public school and a perennial basketball powerhouse. They defeated Gilman School the previous week and had the fastest running back in Baltimore. He scored three touchdowns against Gilman with his speed. Our coach warned us all week in practice to contain him on the playing field or "Katie bar the door." In a great defensive battle, Curley defeated Dunbar and stifled the speed merchant all day. Because of the tightness of the fray and the necessity of keeping the starters in the game, few substitutes played. But Curley won its second consecutive conference game that season.

The next game was against Southern High, a public school from south Baltimore. For the second straight week we played a game at Kirk Field, which was the home field for all Baltimore City public schools that didn't have a stadium. Southern had a bad year and our team desperately needed a laugher. Curley got it, as we led by four touchdowns at halftime. I started on defense in the third quarter. Normally that was great news, but I was ill from drinking Canadian whiskey the previous night. As we had two days off from school, a friend and I drank mixed drinks of Coca Cola and Canadian whiskey. It was stupid and I regretted it. Nevertheless, I entered the game after getting sick in the pre-game warmup drills. On my first play on defense, I overran the offensive guard for Southern and chased their quarterback. When I heard the word *draw*, I realized that it was a fullback draw and met their fullback. He was shorter than me but weighed at least one hundred ninety pounds. He stuck his helmet into my stomach and I grabbed hold of his waist and held on to him for five yards, before we collapsed. I vomited on Kirk Field and the referee asked me "Son, are you all right?" Then our coach yelled from the bench "One hell of a tackle Christopher." But I was sick on my stomach and took a seat on the bench. Drinking alcohol before a game doesn't work. Curley won the game easily and improved our 'B' Conference record with our third straight win and shutout. We were on a roll!

Our next game was the *Baltimore Sunpapers* game of the week. The *Sunpapers* selected a game which had championship overtures and this game definitely fit that definition. The opponent was McDonogh and they had outscored the same three opponents. McDonogh, a private military preparatory school in Baltimore County, had possibly the best quarterback in the MSA and a bone shattering defense, which pitched weekly shutouts against its opponents. McDonogh had been our biggest nemesis the past three years and we had never defeated them in football.

This particular game lived up to all its expectations. Both defenses were flawless and the game remained scoreless until the fourth quarter. We scored first and took a one touchdown lead early in the fourth quarter. But on the ensuing possession McDonogh scored a touchdown as their exceptional quarterback threw four straight completions. This score was the first points yielded by our defense since the Gibbons game, or sixteen straight quarters without allowing a single point. McDonogh's quarterback threw another pass for the two point conversion and a tie game. At this time neither team moved the ball well until two minutes remained in the game and McDonogh moved past midfield and into our territory. The crowd at Curley grew tense and the scenario started to resemble the previous three games that Curley played against McDonogh. The great McDonogh quarterback grew bolder and threw a pass that floated a little too far into the eager hands of our defensive back. He returned the football to midfield and gave the Friars one last chance to win the game with approximately thirty seconds left. After an incomplete pass, our quarterback threw a short pass five yards past the line of scrimmage. Our flanker avoided the McDonogh linebacker with a tremendous move, caught the football, and raced fifty yards for the winning score. The crowd of over a thousand fans at Curley grew louder with each step that our flanker took on the winning touchdown. As he crossed the goal line, the crowd became delirious. With five seconds left in the game, we kicked off to McDonogh, and all eleven of us arrived at the football. There was literally a sea of black on the football field as the game ended and the celebration started. Curley had finally defeated McDonogh. The next day's newspaper revealed that Forest Park had defeated Patterson and was tied at the top of the 'B' Conference standings with us.

Although Forest Park loomed on the horizon in November, we still had another game. That was at home against Gilman. The private non-denominational Ivy League preparatory school had a rebuilding year with mostly sophomores and freshmen starting on the varsity football team. On Halloween we took a quick lead against Gilman and led at halftime. In the second half Gilman scored a touchdown and then Curley answered with another touchdown to take a two touchdown lead at the outset of the fourth quarter. At this point in the game, I had my one shining moment in football. On the succeeding kickoff, the Gilman runner went scurrying up the sideline toward me and faked me out of my shoes, causing me to fall to the ground.

As he reversed direction toward the hash mark on the field, I yanked him down by his ankles from a prone position. Before I arose, he threw the football at me and incurred a fifteen yard penalty for unsportsmanlike conduct. The large throng at Curley became delirious as the referee moved the football back into Gilman territory. I didn't fully realize the ramnifications of this play until a review of that game during the following week. I was the last Curley player between the Gilman ball carrier and the end zone. The crowd acknowledged the play by giving me a standing ovation. After reading the newspaper the next day, I realized that we were alone at the top of the 'B' Conference standings, as Forest Park lost to McDonogh. Curley was undefeated in the 'B' Conference with McDonogh, Forest Park, and Patterson, all tied for second place with one loss apiece. We still had to play both Forest Park and Patterson on the road in November. If we defeated either school, Curley clinched a share of the 'B' Conference championship and its first football crown.

This was one of those times in life, when one hoped that time stood still. We were alone in first place. But of course, time did not stand still and change is the one constant about life. Such was our fate at Curley in November 1969. We practiced hard all week for Saturday's date with Forest Park, whom we knew was tough from our previous year's championship clash. They were a public school from west Baltimore and the defending 'B' Conference football champions. On Friday we had a light workout at Curley and some ventured to Patterson High and watched their game with McDonogh. The loser was eliminated from the 'B' Conference race. To our amazement, Patterson trounced McDonogh to give us a glimpse of our game with them.

That Saturday was a rainy, dreary day with the temperatures hovering near the forty degree mark. On the opening kickoff, we received the football and returned it to the Forest Park twenty yard line, nearly scoring a touchdown on the play. But that play was the last big gainer of the day. We struggled on offense and found ourselves in our own territory on the first set of downs. Due to their aggressive defense and numerous penalties, we went steadily backward. The only significant play took place in the second quarter when we fumbled deep in our own territory. Forest Park moved the football a few yards forward and kicked a field goal for a three point lead. With two outstanding defenses on the field, the three point field goal remained as the only points in the game. Near the end of the game, our offense came to life and moved the football into their territory. But on successive plays, we failed to move the football until fourth down. On a last gasp play, our quarterback threw a perfect strike to our offensive end at the goal line. Their defensive player collided with our player, which produced a penalty flag. Curley had one last flicker of hope when the backfield judge called the penalty against Forest Park. But the head referee overruled him and called it offensive pass interference. Our varsity assistant coach exploded. He kicked one of the benches toward the field, screaming at the head referee "You just cost us the championship". I hoped he was wrong. Curley lost the game and fell into a three way tie for first place with Forest Park and Patterson with one loss apiece.

On Monday after the game, we were all subdued, but realized everything was still at stake in the last game. We couldn't get too disconsolate about our first conference loss, when we still had a chance to win a share of the 'B'

Conference title. Patterson High, our other arch rival, was an east Baltimore public school with the best pair of running backs in the Maryland Scholastic Association that year. That week was labeled championship week for a lot of reasons, and the upcoming game was labeled the *Hail Bowl* and was remembered as one of the greatest high school championships in the MSA. On the other hand, Forest Park had to defeat Southern to win a share of the 'B' Conference title. They easily defeated Southern High and earned a share of the championship.

On Wednesday of that week, Patterson's varsity cross country team won the MSA championship. A friend of mine who worked at the Brentwood Inn was ecstatic, as he was a member of that cross country team. On Thursday, Curley and Patterson vied for the soccer championship at Kirk Field for the third straight year. Patterson won its second team championship in two days by defeating Curley. That left Friday and the football team traveling to the lion's den at Patterson High. Before the game, our players noticed that it was the largest amount of fans that we had ever seen for a high school football game. The weather was forty degrees and overcast as we kicked off to Patterson.

Patterson scored quickly and took a two touchdown lead over our vaunted defense, just five minutes into the game. But Curley mounted a spirited comeback and tied the score by the end of the first quarter. In the second quarter we committed a cardinal error on special teams, allowing Patterson to block one of our punts. Their defensive tackle rambled with the blocked punt sixty yards and provided Patterson with an eight point halftime lead. In the third quarter, Patterson mounted their best offensive drive of the day, scoring a touchdown and adding a two point conversion for a seemingly insurmountable lead heading into the fourth quarter. The pro-Patterson crowd was ecstatic as hail began to fall from the sky. But this game had huge momentum swings as Patterson owned the entire third quarter. But the fourth quarter was different.

Our running back stunned the entire Patterson defense with a sixty yard touchdown run early in the fourth quarter, cutting the lead to ten points. Then I made a good play on the ensuing kickoff. On the sideline I had practiced a spin move and on this particular play, I avoided their blockers. As I closed within eyesight of the ball carrier at the twenty yard line, I was knocked unconscious to the turf. As I arose from the ground, penalty flags were everywhere. The penalty pinned down Patterson's offense at the shadows of their own goalposts. Our defense stiffened and we scored quickly again, cutting the margin to four points. With approximately three minutes left in the game, we executed a perfect onsides kick. We had control of the football and completely hushed the pro-Patterson throng. Our offense rushed the ball extremely well, moving the football to the Patterson six yard line as the two minute warning sounded. After the timeout, our coach opted to throw the football and our quarterback threw to our offensive end in the end zone. He dropped the touchdown pass, but we still had time to win the game. On second down we attempted the same play. This time, Patterson's capable linebacker covered our offensive end better and produced an interception. The game ended and we lost the championship by four points in the hail.

There were a lot of factors that contributed to our demise. Turnovers by us and missed extra point conversions were at the top of my list. Actually both teams scored four touchdowns each in a tremendous championship game. On our return to school, we had to detour through Highlandtown because of damage to the roads caused by the hail. Highlandtown was the area of Baltimore where most of Patterson's student body resided. On every street corner, elderly citizens and Patterson's students screamed "We're Number One" at the Archbishop Curley High School football team bus. By winning three varsity championships in three days. Patterson had stolen our thunder from the previous year. I discovered later that weekend, that my best friend from Loganview Drive, was involved in a tragic automobile accident near the Marine Corps base in California. As this accident also occurred on November 14th, the day just evolved into a disaster.

But life goes on as the old adage says. My best friend recovered from the operation and by Thanksgiving Day, many on Loganview Drive gave thanks to God for his amazing recovery. On the other hand, his wife perished from the damage done to her body in the same accident. My friend had completed a battle tour in Vietnam and had been married for only a brief period of time. As a result of this accident, I decided to make a monetary donation to Curley's *Christmas In Vietnam* fund. The *Christmas In Vietnam* organization at Curley sent packages of food, clothing, and recreational needs to service personnel in Vietnam. Even though my friend never received that particular package, I felt a moral obligation to send a package to someone in Vietnam, on behalf of my friend. At this time life and death issues certainly outweighed any touchy teenage topics, like losing a football championship. One's perspective can quickly change in life.

It took a while to recover, but I finally started to focus on wrestling by the beginning of December. Practice had started in mid-November but I was devastated by my friend's plight and disappointed with the final outcome of the football season. But I was a better wrestler than a football player and this was my final year of high school wrestling. In order to realize my championship dream of 1964, the time for action was now.

If coaches evaluated wrestling teams in preseason like they did in football, Curley would have probably been picked for last in the 'B' Conference. We had twenty-six points in the previous MSA Wrestling Tournament, but almost all of those points were produced by wrestlers who had graduated from high school. Even our tri-captains were not exceptional wrestlers in the previous year. Both our junior 107 pound captain and senior 154 pound captain produced mediocre records in 1969, while our senior 165 pound captain had a winning record at the varsity level of competition. The rest of our wrestling team had less varsity wins. I had only one varsity win from the previous year. But we did have a championship JV wrestling team from the previous year that was undefeated.

There were some major changes that year that directly affected the wrestling team. For a lot of reasons, the administration at Curley decided that the wrestling team would no longer use the cafeteria to practice our daily routine. An agreement was made with Saint Anthony's Parish to use their facilities for our daily wrestling practices. This new practice facility necessitated that the entire team be transported back and forth from Curley, in a three mile direction. Although an imposition to some, it fostered greater friendships among others. Of all the many groups of people that I have ever met, this was truly one of the closest knit groups. Both varsity and junior varsity wrestlers knew each other well. Another change for the upcoming wrestling season was the creation of the 185 pound weight class in MSA competition. It gave two hundred pound football players a chance to shed a few pounds and compete in wrestling. Curley immediately benefited from this additional weight class.

Our first match that wrestling season was at Maryland School for the Blind. Our coach cautioned us about their incredible grip and strength. He was right on both counts. Nevertheless, the Curley Friars demolished Maryland School for the Blind. The highlight for the home team was their heavyweight pinning our heavyweight in the last match. Before that, we had pinned six of their wrestlers, and won all but one individual match. Even I got into the act with my first varsity pin. But for our heavyweight in his varsity match, it was a demoralizing loss. But having been a good football player and a great shot putter on the track and field team, I knew that he would rebound. The following week we demolished Dunbar on their mats. However I got pinned, after taking an early five point lead against my opponent, whom I had wrestled in the previous year. I didn't reverse my pinning hold on him and got rolled onto my back, where my shoulders received a quick one second count. But the wrestling team was undefeated with the onset of the holidays and I was happy about that development.

Between Christmas and New Year's Day 1970, the *Baltimore Sunpapers* went on strike and newspaper circulation ceased for two months. This excellent wrestling team at Curley did not receive any news coverage and is one of the main reasons that I am writing this autobiography. I always felt that the wrestling team during that winter deserved more accolades than we ever received from the media.

Our first match in 1970 was the most difficult one of

the season. Mergenthaler Vocational Tech or Mervo for short usage, had almost every wrestler returning from the previous year's team that annihilated Curley. In addition to that, Mervo had already shutout Northern High School in its initial match of the year, when there was coverage of high school wrestling. Curley's only advantage was that this was our first home match of the year. The crowd was extremely large in anticipation of a great match between two undefeated wrestling schools.

When the match started, two of the best wrestlers at the 107 pound weight class faced each other. Mervo's strongman at that weight defeated our tri-captain and Mervo never looked back. Their 107 pound wrestler bench pressed two hundred and twenty-five pounds in the *Mister Baltimore* contest at a later date. But the rest of Mervo's wrestling team was equally strong. By the time the match progressed to my weight class at 175 pounds, Mervo led by ten points and looked to clinch the match with a victory. Their wrestler was very good and built up a numerical advantage at the start of the final period of the match. But I caught him off balance with an inside switch move and pinned him. The large crowd at Curley erupted, as we cut Mervo's advantage to five points. With an excellent 185 pound wrestler up next and our heavyweight to follow, Curley still had a chance to defeat a powerful wrestling team. But Mervo prevailed due to the efforts of their heaviest wrestlers, whom were very good. For my effort, I was named Curley's 'Wrestler of the Week', which was our wrestling coach's motivational tool. It recognized the wrestler who most contributed to the success of the team during that week and the nominee was posted above the school's glass trophy case. The opponent from Mervo that I pinned, did not lose another match until the MSA wrestling finals at the 175 pound weight class.

The following week's match was at Northern High School. This was the same team that Mervo had destroyed during the previous month. In December, Northern High's two best wrestlers at the two heaviest weight classes did not wrestle against Mervo, due to football injuries. But their wrestling team was healthy now. The match ended in a tie, causing our team's record to remain the same. I improved my overall record with a decision, but did not wrestle well.

The following Friday we traveled to Loyola and wrestled there for the second straight year. Their wrestling team was undefeated, but we were better and gave them their first loss. Actually our team wrestled well and we prevailed easily. I lost my second match of the year and this time, it was against an opponent whom I had defeated during the previous year. But he caught me in a takedown during the first thirty seconds of the match and put me on my back briefly for a quick advantage. I later rebounded with a two point reversal in the third period and earned a riding time point, but still lost the match by decision. I made a promise after this match to never lose again. However the wrestling team improved our overall record to three wins, a loss and a tie.

Curley did not have another match until the end of January at Friends School, a private Quaker school in northern Baltimore. In front of a sparse crowd, we pinned them quickly, taking only thirty-eight minutes to do so. I wrestled at the heavyweight class, pinning their 230 pound wrestler to put an exclamation point on the match. We were jubilant about our success, until our JV coach scolded us, saying that Mervo took only twenty-two minutes to finish eleven individual matches with Friends School. And so the season's beat went on as our team improved to four wins one loss and one tie entering February, and still trailed unbeaten Mervo in the 'B' Conference race.

Our next match on February 2nd was our second home match of the year. We wrestled Northwestern, a public school from northwestern Baltimore City. The raucous crowd at Curley got louder by day's end. Our new 145 pound wrestler lost, who was undefeated at the 154 pound weight class before the match, and Northwestern led us by seven points, when my match began. I nearly pinned my opponent in the first period and held a commanding lead. Nineteen seconds into the second period, I pinned my opponent, cutting Northwestern's lead to two points. Our 165 pound wrestler followed with a quick pin, putting Curley in front by three points. But the new 175 pound wrestler got pinned, allowing Northwestern to regain the advantage. But Curley's 185 pounder and heavyweight pinned the opposition and provided the final points for our win. The team was five wins one loss and a tie with two matches left in the season.

That same night, I worked at the Brentwood Inn and was happy about the big wrestling win. That night one of the waitresses discovered that her husband was cheating on her. I didn't know why this waitress came to work, except to elicit sympathy from her co-workers. I was attracted to this voluptuous thirty-year old with auburn hair and hated to see her cry. As I was the *closing* busboy and she was the *closing* waitress, she asked me to walk her to her home, a short distance from the Brentwood Inn. After she asked me to come inside her home, one thing led to another and soon we were in her bed, making love to each other. She asked me if I was a virgin and I denied it. However I became eighteen years of age at the stroke of midnight on February 3rd and was therefore a consenting adult. About 5 A.M., my new friend awakened me and asked me about school that day. Of course I had school, and immediately ran three blocks to hail a taxicab and make a quick exodus to my home, which was two miles away from my friend's house. Upon arrival I opened the front door and saw my mother descending the stairs. She wanted to know where I had been, and I told her that I had fallen asleep at a friend's house, which was half the truth. Then mom informed me that she had made some pancakes with butter and syrup for my birthday. Needless to say, this became one of the best birthdays that I've ever enjoyed in my life.

That day in school, I smiled in every class and at every teacher. Even my wrestling buddies needled me about being so happy after another big win. I was happy but I wanted more of everything. I asked my new friend many times for a date without any success. I even asked her to attend my last wrestling match of the season, but she refused my offer. I always looked upon this 'one night stand' as a friend helping a friend through a trying ordeal in one's life. For that one night, we were the two best friends that each other had in the whole world.

Friday's match during that week was against our chief nemesis at Patterson High. It had been three months since the football team visited there and it was time for revenge. They had three undefeated wrestlers at the 138, 154 and 165 pound weight classes. Curley had one loss as a team and an undefeated 165 pound wrestler. By the time my match commenced at the 154 pound weight class, we had a nice lead. I squared off with their all MSA running back and an undefeated wrestler. In a great match, I outlasted him by one point and ended his undefeated season. In the match of two undefeated wrestlers, their 165 pound wrestler ended our undefeated wrestler's season by a narrow decision. In a tough dual meet with two testy rivals, Curley prevailed and gained a measure of revenge for the previous events of the fall season. Moreover in eleven individual matches between two great rivals, no pins were recorded. Patterson still had two undefeated wrestlers, but we had the victory. This was Curley's first victory against Patterson in varsity wrestling. For my efforts against Northwestern and Patterson, I was again selected as Curley's 'Wrestler of the Week'.

Our final match of the year was against Saint Paul's Episcopalian School at home. Curley had never defeated them in a wrestling meet, but this group of Curley wrestlers was rewriting history. We were six wins one loss and one tie as a team, which was the best winning percentage in wrestling in the school's history. We had winners in almost every weight class and we had a noisy crowd as well. Saint Paul's wrestling team, which was usually tough, came to Curley as an unknown quantity, due to lack of any newspaper coverage. As our lightweight wrestlers had done all year, they defeated Saint Paul's lightweights, and by the time the match proceeded to my weight class, the outcome was decided. With two pins in two matches at home already that year, the crowd grew restless in anticipation of a third and final pin. My worthwhile opponent held me in check in a scoreless tie beginning my last two minute period at home. As the last period began, I scored a two point reversal in two seconds and pushed my opponent onto his back. Then I sank a half nelson deep into his neck, putting him squarely on his back. The crowd grew noisier but to no avail. I won the match by decisive decision and Curley easily defeated Saint Paul's School for the first time in our school's brief wrestling history. However I was mildly disappointed that my lady friend didn't attend the match and also that I didn't record my third straight pin at home. My wrestling foe from Saint Paul's told some of Curley's wrestlers in 1971 that the last two minutes of his match with me were the longest two minutes of his life. It is little wonder with a thousand fans banging their feet on the floorboards of the gymnasium. The team finished the season with the best overall record in Curley's wrestling history with seven wins, one loss and one tie. We had nearly two weeks to prepare for the Maryland Scholastic Association Wrestling Tournament.

Sometimes social events ruin the natural flow of progress in life. During this time Curley's wrestling team became the victim of this type of situation. The third week of February was set aside for an 'A' Conference dual meet wrestling championship match and a 'B' Conference dual meet wrestling championship match. Without a newspaper providing reliable news in the Baltimore area at that time, we had heard that there was racial unrest at Baltimore's City College High School, which had a large black student population. Their arch rival Baltimore Polytechnic Institute, had a majority of white students, and a wrestling team that was undefeated in the 'A' Conference. Poly and undefeated City were scheduled to wrestle for the 'A' Conference wrestling championship that week. But the match was cancelled and bitter rivals City and Poly, were declared 'A' Conference co-champions. In the 'B' Conference, the social unrest in Baltimore City, created an even worse scenario for Curley's wrestling team. We had discovered that since the start of wrestling season, the 'B' Conference was divided into Division I and Division II, because of the large number of wrestling schools in the conference. Curley was lumped into

Division I with Mergenthaler Vocational Technical School or Mervo, whose wrestling team was undefeated. Loyola was the best wrestling school in Division II, having lost their only match to Curley. Because Mervo had a racially mixed population and Loyola had an overwhelmingly white population, the Maryland Scholastic Association declared these two schools as 'B' Conference co-champions, without a championship match to decide the winner. There is still a pennant at Loyola High School signifying this championship.

Our wrestling team at Curley was frustrated. We had defeated Loyola on their own mats at the castle, but lost to social unrest for a conference championship. It still upsets me to this day about the sequence of events during that particular week in February 1970. Meanwhile we practiced hard for the upcoming wrestling tournament, preparing to show the Maryland Scholastic Association how good Curley's wrestling team was in an unreported season of events.

Seeding was done for this tournament as in any tournament according to the wrestlers' individual records. The better the seed, like a first or second, the better the individual wrestler's record had been. Curley had eight of eleven wrestlers seeded in the top eight of their respective weight classes for the MSA Wrestling Tournament that year. Only Polytechnic Institute had more seeds with nine. City College High School equaled Curley's amount. We had one fifth seed, two sixth seeds, two seventh seeds, and three eighth seeds in the MSA Wrestling Tournament in 1970. The bad news is that none of our wrestlers was seeded in the top four of his weight class. I was a sixth seed in the 154 pound weight class, but I was dismayed at the seeds. The best wrestler in my weight class from Mervo, who happened to be black, was seeded second. This agonizing fact meant that I could not wrestle him in the championship finals, part of my 1964 wrestling dream. If we faced each other, it would be in the semi-finals. But he and I met later in an even bigger arena.

The opening round of the tournament was Wednesday and ended Saturday with the championship finals. I was one of a few wrestlers that wrestled in the opening round on Wednesday. I pinned my unseeded opponent from Friends School in the first period of the match. Curley had its first two points of the MSA tournament and I improved my overall record to eight wins and two losses for the year. But Thursday was the day of Curley's demise. Nearly all of our wrestlers lost, including two of our three tri-captains, both of whom had one loss for the entire season. Actually Patterson High School, our arch rival, had its entire wrestling team eliminated from the MSA tournament for being late for the team's weigh-in. Since my unseeded opponent from Patterson was declared ineligible to wrestle, I was awarded a forfeit, advancing to the MSA quarterfinals on Friday. Curley received two more points and I won my sixth straight wrestling match to improve to nine wins and two losses for the season. I now had the most wins of any senior on this wrestling team.

By the MSA quarterfinals, Curley had only four wrestlers remaining. We had our junior tri-captain at 107 pounds, a great junior wrestler at 115 pounds, me at 154 pounds, and our senior heavyweight. Our heavyweight did a great job, for someone who had never wrestled before that year. But the bubble burst for all but one, that day at Community College of Baltimore. Our 115 pound wrestler, a native of Dundalk, prevailed in both matches on Friday and reached the championship finals on Saturday. He lost in the finals to his City College opponent and tied for the second best record on the team with a nine win and three loss record. Our junior 107 pound wrestler finished in fourth place in his weight class and led the entire Curley team with ten wins and four losses. Meanwhile I got crushed by Gilman's 154 pound wrestler in the quarterfinals. The Gilman wrestler placed fourth in the 154 pound weight class, behind the champion from Mervo. The champion easily demolished his opponent from Loyola in the finals. I had the right champion as a part of my wrestling dream, but I wasn't a part of that dream. I finished my senior season with a nine win and three loss record, the same record as our championship finalist at 115 pounds. But I would have gladly exchanged places with him on the podium. Nevertheless he earned that silver trophy by having a great tournament. Our heavyweight was also eliminated Friday afternoon after his previous day's win and finished the season with a record of six wins and four losses.

Curley finished the tournament with twenty points for a disappointing tenth place finish out of twenty-three schools. Gilman from the 'A' Conference with seven seeds, won the MSA Wrestling Tournament by fending off feisty 'B' Conference power Mervo, also with seven seeds. There were some great matches in the championship finals between these two wrestling powers, but Gilman won most of them to win the team trophy.

By March 1970 the key question for me was how to get a college scholarship. Now that wrestling season ended, would this senior *late bloomer* earn a college scholarship? The wrestling coach at Loyola College offered me a quarter of a scholarship to wrestle at that school. But with tuition there at $1500 per semester, three fourths of that sum was a considerable amount and my parents could not afford that. The following week Frostburg State College offered me a full football scholarship, but when they discovered that I was only 5 foot 8 inches tall and 175 pounds, they withdrew the offer. But the school reminded me that I was welcome to play football, just without a scholarship. But wrestling was my first choice, and since Frostburg State didn't have a wrestling program, I had no interest in attending that school.

My grades plummeted during my senior year from the low 90th percentile to the mid 80th percentile which was a B minus average at Curley. This dropped my place in class standing from 28th out of 278 students in my junior year to 63rd out of 253 students at the conclusion of my senior year. But I was still the last student in the top 25% of my class academically. With all of the true geniuses in my class, it is amazing that I finished that high in the pecking order. When I started to believe that college was taboo, mom came to the rescue as she always did for her kids.

My mother Alma worked for four years at Fort Holabird as a personnel records clerk and while there, discovered some information about Maryland state scholarships for college. Our state senator from Dundalk was satisfied with my high school academic file and the rest was history. The new question became, where would I go to college? All of the local colleges had already accepted me as a student except Johns Hopkins University. Due in large part to Archbishop Curley's fine staff of dedicated teachers, I decided that teaching was my career goal. The best teachers' college in the state of Maryland was Towson State College, and with tuition at three hundred dollars plus tax per semester, it was an economic bargain for me. The scholarship amount was three hundred dollars per semester or two thousand four hundred dollars paid by the state for four years attendance at college. The effort was entirely up to me. After I graduated from high school on June 4th 1970 at the Cathedral of Mary Our Queen, my immediate future was set. As most of my classmates departed in different directions, our paths seldom crossed again. But I felt that all of us at that school became better, more independent Christians due to the unceasing efforts of the fine teaching staff at Archbishop Curley High School. They saved my life and prepared me for a future in the real world.

Chapter IV

ATTENDING A CO-EDUCATIONAL
COLLEGE AND A CHAMPIONSHIP TROPHY

I f the summer of 1969 produced some major waves in my life, the summer of 1970 produced a deadly tsunami. Thanks to uncle Sam Denes, I worked my first full time job at Bethlehem Steel in the tin mill that summer. At least I worked ten straight weeks in the summer program for college students. At that time uncle Sam had been an electrician for Bethlehem Steel for fifteen years and succeeded in getting me and his son Sam Junior, an hourly job for the summer. My uncle eventually retired after forty years at Bethlehem Steel and now lives in Stuart, Florida with my aunt Dorothy by his side.

In 1970 my cousin Sammy started his sophomore year at Harford Community College in Harford County, Maryland where he resided with uncle Sam and aunt Dot, my mother's sister. I have always been appreciative of the many efforts made by mom's side of the family in my behalf, in helping me to remain gainfully employed during college.

While still catching buses to work, I took a single eight hour course of driving instruction and on June 18th, passed the driver's test and received a driver's license. I looked at the calendar and realized that just two weeks before that, I had graduated from high school. That Friday night, I drove my mother's car, a 1964 Rambler, to the carnival at Sacred Heart of Jesus Church in celebration of this milestone achievement. I only allowed one tire to go over the curb while parking mom's car there.

During the next two months I worked at Bethlehem Steel, caught the bus, and brought my checks home. Mom occasionally let me drive her car. One slippery day in late July, I ran over a curb, with the entire car doing thirty-five miles per hour on Broening Highway in Baltimore. The tires were worn and although the posted speed limit was thirty-five miles per hour, it was twenty miles per hour on the curves of the road which I overran. Mom was furious when she discovered that her car's axle was broken, but she had the car fixed. Even though I had learned another harsh lesson, mom did not permit me to drive her 1964 Rambler for a while.

Dad did not allow me to drive his 1968 Pontiac Ventura convertible until we took our last family vacation to Ocean City in August. Then in his presence, he let me check out the passing gear on this sleek, purple automobile on the eastern shore of Maryland. Shortly thereafter, I saw a police car with blue light flashing, and was pulled over for speeding. The policeman said that I was driving ninety-one miles per hour in a sixty mile per hour speed zone according to radar. He gave me a break, as this was my first traffic offense and wrote a ticket for exceeding the posted speed limit by more than ten miles per hour. Dad said "Move over and let me drive. You need to pay that ticket and whatever you do, don't go to traffic court." He was right and I learned another lesson. My parents really loved me to pay the extra automobile insurance and car damage that they incurred from my poor driving habits. Nevertheless I actually survived to attend Towson State College's freshmen orientation in August 1970.

Towson State College had been an advanced institution for higher learning since 1866. In previous years it had been named Maryland State Normal School and State Teachers' College at Towson. By 1970 it was called Towson State College and with six thousand full time undergraduate students, it was a work in progress. The student enrollment and the campus space steadily increased during my four years on campus. Towson had an extensive liberal arts curriculum with many majors of study, but was best known for teaching certification, at both the elementary and secondary education levels. The college had many classroom buildings and student dormitories along with parking facilities, and occupied about two square miles of property north of York Road in Towson. It took me about a month before I could properly navigate around the large campus.

As I began my freshman year of college, I had four very distinct goals for the next four years. In order of priority, the first goal was to obtain a bachelor's degree and teaching certification, and to teach in the subject of my major field of study. The second goal was to stay gainfully employed in some capacity during the entire college stint. This meant alternating employment between Brentwood Inn and whatever summer employment that became available. My third goal was to wrestle on a championship team and wrestle for an individual conference championship. Finally I wished to develop a relationship with a member of the opposite sex. All of these goals were possible and all required significant effort.

During my first week of classes, I became mesmerized by a figure and involved with new found friendships. In Introduction to Speech class that week, a young lady with an expansive bust line and without a brassiere caught my lengthy leer. My speech professor then asked me if I was okay. Stammering, I muttered something about finally making it to heaven. At that moment my tongue-in-cheek professor replied "When you finish this course, you may think that you went to another place."

Another class that I took that first semester was English Composition and Conversation. Our professor from England was arrogant and rude but grammatically correct about the English language. Two new male friends, who I met at freshman orientation, were in the same class and both graduated from Baltimore Polytechnic Institute. For the initial assignment, each student was required to submit a composition about one's summer exploits. In the next English class, our professor expressed his displeasure with lack of composition skills in our particular class. He then chose to read the poor essays aloud and to my immediate embarrassment, I realized that the first paper read was mine. The professor threw the composition at my desk and gave me an F minus for the paper. Then he read another composition and gave one of my new friends an F minus minus and threw his paper at him. The third composition was also read aloud, assigned a grade of F minus minus minus and thrown to the floor in front of my other new friend. The paper remained on the floor. All three of us bonded from that moment and despised our English professor with equal passion.

The amazing thing about this new friendship was that all three of us played key roles in Towson State College's history. My one friend became senior class president at Towson State, majored in English, graduated with a bachelor's degree, and became an English teacher at the middle school level. My other friend was the Student Government Association president at Towson State College during the turbulent 1970s. And I became a fairly decent college wrestler during the next few years. All three of us remained friends after graduation.

As far as college wrestling was concerned, I heard that Towson State College had a coach that most considered one tough dude. I met the wrestling coach during the second week of September and inquired about wrestling. He was maybe five foot seven inches tall and one hundred fifty pounds soaking wet with dirty blonde hair, long sideburns and a pipe smoker. He informed me that I was late for preseason conditioning. I stated that high school practice didn't even start until November 15th. Coach just glared at me and stated that college practice started October 15th and that if I wasn't running two miles before practice, that I would *never be in condition* to wrestle that year. He then handed me a preseason conditioning schedule that began September 10th with a mile run and ended on October 14th with a 2 ½ mile run before wrestling season officially started. He spun around quickly and said "You're already behind everyone else on the team as it is September 15th and you haven't run a single step." Needless to say I was in for a rude awakening, as I only half-heartedly took his advice. By the end of the first official week of practice, I realized the severity of physical conditioning in preparation for college wrestling. Coach was a genius in his daily conditioning regimen. We lifted weights one day for strength improvement and worked on speed repetitions the next day. To this day, I still follow this regimen in my daily exercise routine. Pushups on a daily basis ended for me when our college coach showed us a better way.

In the interim I continued work as a busboy at the Brentwood Inn, due to the intercession of the head busboy there who was a Curley alumnus. My grades at Towson State were shaky, but I earned a C+ average and 12 ½ credits after the first semester of college studies. Depite my worst intentions, my English professor passed me with a D grade. His reasoning was simple, like him. He said "I don't want you to retake this course in any of my distinguished colleague's classes." I received a C grade from my speech professor and he jokingly asked "Had I gone to Hades?" I told him no, but as a practicing Catholic I believed in purgatory, and his class was probably in the middle of it. He chuckled at this idea. I thought that he was a good professor because of his dogged determination to have students learn what he taught in class. Most of my professors at Towson State College were dedicated professionals like my speech and communications professor. My English professor was unique, thank God.

By Thanksgiving wrestling became front page sports news, as it was a winter sport. The wrestling team in college, referred to as the starting team, were all sophomores and upper classmen. The year 1970 to 1971 was the last year that freshmen were prohibited from starting on the wrestling team, or any other varsity college sport. But Towson State had a freshmen wrestling team and I started at the 158 pound weight class for all five freshmen matches that year. Overall I did a good job during that particular year.

Our first freshmen wrestling match that season was against Catonsville Community College at home. Catonsville won the Maryland Community College Wrestling Tournament later that year so they had a very good team. By the time the match proceeded to my weight class, Towson was losing badly but I ended the shutout. I defeated my opponent by decision and scored the team's first points in the match. Later that season my Catonsville foe placed second in his weight class at the community college tournament. Towson State's freshman heavyweight from Towson High School won our second individual match of the ten matches wrestled, but Catonsville Community College easily won.

The next match of the season was held on a week day against Nassau Community College of Long Island, New York. This match was scheduled the week before final exams and was at Towson. In fact all of our freshmen wrestling team's matches were at home. Nassau had already won three matches when they ventured to Towson, and their 158 pound wrestler, was the most muscular wrestler that I had ever seen. My only hope was that he might not be very fast or intelligent as a wrestler. I guessed wrong on both counts. Our 126 pound wrestler was the only Towson winner until my match. I was taken down in the first period and nearly pinned. In fact the rest of the match I expended considerable effort to keep from getting pinned. This was my worst defeat by decision ever. As bad as I felt about my individual match, Towson's freshman team fared worse, losing all but the one match to Nassau Community College. Later my opponent pinned all of his opponents throughout the year, except for me and one other in dual meet matches. He became the National Junior College Tournament wrestling champion at the 158 pound weight class in 1971. This was not the last national champion that I wrestled on the mats.

Our last freshmen match of 1970 on the Friday before final

examinations was against the Naval Academy plebes. Their wrestling coach was nationally renowned and their wrestling team was usually ranked in the top twenty ranked wrestling schools annually, so we thought the plebes were good. Despite the possibility of losing our third straight freshmen wrestling team match at home, our 142 pounder and I got into a crazy, friendly wager before the match. Since we both had to starve to make weight for the match, we decided on a submarine eating contest. We each bought a regular sized submarine and whoever ate their submarine the fastest, the other wrestler had to reimburse him for the cost of his submarine. We both made weight, but my buddy from Overlea High School ate his steak submarine in one minute thirty seconds, while it took me ten seconds longer to finish my crab cake submarine. I had to pay him four dollars for the wager, but by the end of the day I got the better end of the bargain.

While all of this food was consumed, our freshmen coach, who was six foot tall and over two hundred pounds, became furious at both of us when he heard about our bet. When my 142 pound buddy began vomiting all over the wrestling mats and the referees stopped the match by default, he demanded that I talk to him at once. He told me "I will kick your butt all over the mat" if I embarrassed him like that. When I took the mat, we were losing badly with a solitary tie for Towson in all of the wrestled matches. My opponent, who was at least six foot tall and thinner than I, immediately took an early lead and was in command of the match. I caught him off balance in the third period with my inside switch move, and forced his back toward the mat. Knowing that I had to pin him or else, I pinned my Naval Academy opponent to trim their lead over us. As I exited the mat, my coach looked at me and said "You are so lucky." I just smiled and said "I am a winner." Unfortunately this match was the last highlight of the day for Towson State and we lost the match badly. But our starting wrestling team at Towson State that year was a very different story from our woeful freshmen team.

In December 1970, the Towson State Tigers with our wonderful school colors of gold and black, mauled all of the Washington D.C. colleges in wrestling. Towson defeated Gallaudet University, American University, and Catholic University easily, with a very talented team comprised of mostly county champions throughout the state of Maryland. Towson was a member of the Mason Dixon Conference, which was a confederation of colleges throughout the Maryland, Washington D.C., and Virginia areas. Gallaudet and Catholic Universities of the above listed colleges were conference members, and thus counted as conference victories. The other colleges in the Mason Dixon Conference were Baltimore University, Loyola College, Western Maryland College, Washington College, University of Maryland at Baltimore County, George Mason University and Hampden Sydney College.

Some observers at Towson said that our annual wrestling match with Johns Hopkins University counted in the conference dual meet standings. However Johns Hopkins never participated in the Mason Dixon Conference wrestling tournament while I attended Towson. But it did not matter how many schools were in our conference, as our coach opted to wrestle only the minimum amount of matches necessary to compete for the Mason Dixon Conference dual meet trophy. The rest of the schedule included tough Pennsylvania schools, where our wrestling coach learned his skills. His reasoning was simple, in that tougher competition made one a better wrestler.

By January 1971, Towson State's wrestling team continued their winning ways in the conference, culminating with a close victory over tough Western Maryland College in Westminster Maryland. This victory assured our wrestling team a perfect record in the conference, winning the Mason Dixon Conference dual meet trophy. However, Western Maryland College got its revenge and won the conference tournament wrestling trophy in February. Nevertheless Towson State sent several wrestlers during that year to the Division III National Wrestling Tournament for winning their respective weight classes in the conference tournament.

Fortunately for us, the freshmen team only had two matches left for the season, Community College of Baltimore and Baltimore University freshmen. Community College of Baltimore had a fairly tough team that year, finishing second to Catonsville Community College in the Maryland JuCo wrestling tournament. Our new 126 pound wrestler from Overlea High School, who had tried out for the team in January, won the only match for us when the match reached the 167 pound weight class. Their 167 pound wrestler and I were in a scoreless tie entering the last period of the match. I made a mistake in the last thirty seconds, nearly getting pinned, and lost the match by decision. The score itself did not get any closer and we lost our fourth straight match of the season at home. My opponent of that day placed second in the Maryland Junior College tournament at that weight class. I lost my second match but redemption was near.

Baltimore University came to Towson State with half a team, starting only five wrestlers in ten weight classes. Towson

State and I won by forfeit. I finished the season with a winning record, being the only freshman at Towson State to do that in all five matches wrestled. Our new wrestler from Overlea finished undefeated with two wins, but was more interested in soccer and lacrosse. My sole interest in college sports was wrestling, even if it was unpopular by most standards.

But in order to continue to compete at any sport, one's grades needed to be at a C average. I had a dismal 2.22 grade point average or GPA after the first semester, with only 12 ½ semester hours earned credit. I needed to improve my grades in the second semester, but with Introduction to Biology looming in my immediate future, it did not look very promising. But at the Harrison home in Dundalk the outlook was anything but gloomy.

In August 1970, President Nixon signed the Postal Reorganization Act, which placed the US Postal Service directly under control of the executive branch of government. The days of the US Post Office under Congressional control had ended. This change in control affected my father and family in a positive manner. When the ramnifications of the law became fully understood, it represented a sweeping salary increase for all postal workers. My dad's salary increased from a little over six dollars an hour to nearly ten dollars per hour in a few months. My dad was happy, as he just received the biggest pay increase in his life at a whopping fifty per cent. Although President Nixon was unpopular in America for a number of reasons, he remained my dad's favorite president until my father died.

With income on the rise at the Harrison household, I asked my dad "When can I have a car?" His answer was blunt. He said "When you work and save your money, you can buy one. I won't stop you. In addition to you, I have three other children to raise." Well I continued to work at the Brentwood Inn without a car. I hoped to own a car in the near future.

With my grades at college heading down a slippery slope, I heard about a one day wrestling tournament at Towson State, available to all wrestlers from ages sixteen to sixty. The AAU sponsored the South Atlantic Wrestling Tournament there, with Greco-Roman wrestling rules. Each period of the match started in the neutral position meaning takedowns were critical to win a match. As takedowns were the weakest part of my game, I decided to enter the tournament. There were no team results as it was based on individual scores. At the end of wrestling season in March, I weighed over one hundred seventy pounds and wrestled at the 177 pound weight class. In a weight class of seven wrestlers, I managed to place third and earned a bronze medal. The champion of the 177 pound weight class was the Mason Dixon Conference wrestling champion from Western Maryland College. He defeated me in the semi-finals by a close decision. It was not the last time that our two paths collided on the mat. But I was happy about my performance in this particular tournament. I got my first medal and was hungry for more. But my performance in the classroom was anything but good.

My grades in the spring semester plummeted due to my D grade in biology. My professor was a good teacher, but I was a poor student. Although I passed the course, my grade point average for the spring semester was 1.96, which meant that I had just a 2.09 GPA for freshman year, or nine hundredths of a point above passing for all the subjects that I had taken that year. But the summer of 1971 was beginning and I was ready for a change.

That summer my uncle Sam Denes came through as he helped my cousin Sammy and me obtain summer jobs at Bethlehem Steel again. Like the summer of 1970 I worked in the tin mill, helping laborers to do all kinds of messy jobs. But labor unrest was brewing that summer at Bethlehem Steel. By the second week of July, the AFL-CIO which championed the causes of all steel workers' unions, struck for better wages and benefits. As the college students were a temporary labor force and labor became unnecessary, management curtailed all college student employment during that particular summer. Of course that ended my summer savings for an automobile plan. But I had a move to make and I needed to do it now.

A famous restaurant owner from Ocean City Maryland had visited Brentwood Inn that spring and complimented the management on how well trained the two busboys were that worked the floor that night. The two busboys in question were the head busboy and me. The restaurant owner was Mister Phillips, who owned Phillips Restaurant on 21st Street in Ocean City. He told the two of us "If either of you ever need a job, look me up." Well in July I needed a job, called his restaurant, and spoke to the hostess there. The following day, Mister Phillips telephoned me and asked me "to come on down." That was an offer that I did not refuse.

I finally ventured out on my own away from my parents at the tender age of nineteen. Both of my parents thought it was a good idea for me to get away from home, but thought that I needed to save money that summer. I left Baltimore with a bus ticket, a suitcase of clothes, and one hundred dollars in my wallet in July. When I returned home on Labor Day weekend, I had the same things except for the bus ticket. But I had changed during those six weeks. I worked, ate, partied and played flag football for Phillips Restaurant. I met some new friends, both male and female, and had a one night stand with a female friend. Generally I just had a blast during the summer of 1971. As for the automobile savings plan, that was not in my foreseeable future. I was temporarily dependent on public transportation, rides from friends, and rides from wrestling teammates. That was how sophomore year at Towson State began.

There were a lot of changes that fall at college, beginning with the construction of a thirteen story dormitory. Each gender had alternating floors until and including the thirteenth floor. Towson expanded its premises and the student population was steadily growing. There were wholesale changes for the wrestling team as well.

In 1971 the NCAA Rules Committee declared that all freshmen could compete in varsity sports from the Division I level down to and including the NAIA level. This impacted Towson State in a very positive manner in wrestling. We had three incoming freshmen who started on the wrestling team and contributed immensely to the team's success.

A second change in wrestling involved the points system for each individual match. To instill more aggression in the sport, more points were awarded for defeating one's opponent by a greater margin. The old system was five team points for pin, default or forfeit, and three team points for a decision, regardless of the score. The new scoring system assigned six team points for a pin, default, or forfeit. A default by definition is when one or both wrestlers cannot continue the match because an injury occurs during the course of the match. By defeating one's opponent by twelve points or more, one received five team points for a superior decision, as it became known.

By defeating one's opponent by a margin of eight to eleven points, one received four team points for a major decision, as it became known. Riding time, when one wrestler controls his opponent by a minute or more, was reduced in value. Before this ruling, if you controlled your opponent by two minutes or more, you received two points. The new rules awarded one point only for riding time, regardless of the amount of riding time one wrestler had over another. A decision of seven points or less remained as three team points awarded to the winner. Ties during an individual match counted the same.

With all of these changes in hand, wrestling practice began in October 1971. The only advantage that I had over the incoming freshmen, was that I had one year experience in our wrestling coach's system. But the new freshmen were very talented wrestlers.

But while wrestling, academics, and work absorbed my time, a terrible tragedy occurred in November, that devastated my mother's family. My cousin Sammy died at twenty years of age in an automobile accident. This was my aunt Dorothy and uncle Sam's only child and it ruined their world. The rest of the family including me were in a state of shock. At this juncture I began to hate the month of November. President John F. Kennedy was assassinated during that month in 1963, my best friend nearly died during that month in 1969, and my cousin died in 1971. Sammy was within one month of completing his associate's degree at Harford Community College. I was proud of my aunt and uncle for weathering this destructive tsunami, and living to the present day. In 1971 though, all of the family members grieved through the holidays.

I returned to practice after Thanksgiving in a daze, but somehow managed to start wrestling again. Towson State's third match was against Gallaudet University, and although I wasn't scheduled to start, our wrestling coach insisted that I travel with the team to Washington D.C. Our lightweights destroyed Gallaudet with numerous six point pins and we had a huge point advantage when the match proceeded to the 167 pound weight class. The regular Towson starter and I were standing near the mat. The Gallaudet wrestler touched the inner circle and I put my foot on the mat. Our coach became visibly upset, then told me that I had to wrestle or we would have to forfeit this individual match. Although I disobeyed our coach's instructions, I still won the match by a close decision. This decision was not only my first varsity win, but officially my first Mason Dixon Conference win as well. During freshmen season I did count the forfeit against Baltimore University as an initial conference win, as that school was a member of the conference at the time. Towson State completed the wrestling demolition of Gallaudet University. With the Tigers routing Catholic University and U.M.B.C. in wrestling during the previous week, Towson State was definitely on a prowl.

Our final match before the holidays was against Gettysburg College in Pennsylvania. The repercussions of this match were discussed for years. Because of failure to follow instructions in the Gallaudet match, I was relegated to freshmen team status for the last time in my career. The freshmen team for Towson State won the match, and I defeated my opponent. Then our starting team took the mats and were easily leading Gettysburg, until the match reached the 190 pound weight class, which was the next to last match of the dual meet. Our 190 pound wrestler who was one of the best on the team, was pinning their wrestler, when pandemonium broke out on the mat. Our 190 pound wrestler stood up, pulled his wrestling top off, and showed the referee his opponent's teeth marks on his exposed ribs. The referee said something to our wrestler like "Just wrestle and forget about it." The crowd which was boisterous at the onset of the match grew belligerent. While sitting with the freshmen team in the front of the stands, I was unclear as to who threw what at whom. Before I knew what happened, objects were hurled at our wrestling team. By now the freshmen team and the starting team were evacuated into the visitors' locker room. As we tried to gather our thoughts, many objects and insults were hurled at the locked door. The wrestling team dressed quickly and we had a Pennsylvania State Police escort to the Maryland state line, which was just seven miles away. Many years after the Battle of Gettysburg in 1863, Towson State College won its battle with Gettysburg College's wrestling team in 1971.

After final examinations ended and the family finished Christmas, my father intercepted my college report card in the mail. He confronted me with this discovery and said "You need to get your butt to work or your body might go to Vietnam." The draft was still strong, but I had a student deferment or 1-H status. But dad's words of caution were helpful. I had only passed thirty-six credit hours after three semesters of study, which was the minimum amount of hours needed to retain my scholarship. To end this academic predicament, I declared a major field of study. In the middle of my sophomore year, I opted for social science as a major. This discipline included a broad field of studies like history, geography, economics, anthropology and sociology. It was the field that was the most interesting to me. Now I took dad's advice and hit the books harder.

With the beginning of the year 1972 and the approaching

of spring semester, I experienced major changes. Since the wrestling team was undefeated, our coach gave the team a week off after the first of the year. I believed the reason that our coach did this was that he had his own vacation plans. But he cautioned all of us to practice somewhere in order to be physically prepared for the rest of the season. I worked out with the wrestling team at Dundalk High School, as their heavyweight was a friend from work. I walked through the school after wrestling practice and spotted a cute brunette with whom I had a conversation. We were attracted to one another, and dated intermittently for the next three years. I finally found a girlfriend. Soon I returned to wrestling practice at Towson State with an occasional date elsewhere.

The wrestling team continued its winning ways, hosting a quadrangular meet with three other teams and defeated all three of these colleges easily. Towson State College defeated Monmouth College of New Jersey, King's College and Rhode Island. I practiced for this meet but did not attend. By the third week of January, *Wrestling News Magazine* listed Towson State College's wrestling team as the eighteenth best in Division III of the NCAA. Being ranked eighteenth in the country was a great honor in 1972, as there were over two hundred and fifty colleges that wrestled at the Division III level. But the prestige of a national ranking was short lived for Towson State.

In late January York College of Pennsylvania visited the undefeated, nationally ranked Towson State Tigers and burst our bubble badly. We lost each individual match by decision and were shutout by the visitors. I observed the match personally and was in a state of shock. Although our coach complained about a lack of aggressiveness, York College was a very tough wrestling team. It was after that match that I received an opportunity to start for the wrestling team. One of our starters transferred to another school and another wrestler became academically ineligible for the spring semester. I was ready, willing, and able to give the team my best shot.

My first match at the end of January was against George Washington University at home. By the time the 167 pound weight class match started, Towson State had already clinched the victory. While wrestling my adversary, I began an outside switch move, then reversed my hips and performed an inside switch. As my arm reached across to his hip, I heard a loud crack. I stopped moving and immediately noticed my opponent writhing in pain on the mat. I realized that I had broken his arm. As my move from the referee's position was legal, I was awarded a six point default, as my opponent was unable to continue the wrestling match. Towson State prevailed again, but I didn't want to win in that manner again. The following Saturday was two days after my birthday, and our wrestling team ventured through Baltimore to Johns Hopkins University with their glass case of forty national championship lacrosse trophies. I struggled in my match at the 167 pound weight class, but the Tigers routed the Blue Jays. The wrestling team had only one loss and I was undefeated at this point of my sophomore season. Since freshman year I had won five straight matches and hadn't lost an individual match in over a year. But all of this changed during the second week of February, when Towson State College traveled to Baltimore University.

Baltimore University with its low ceiling gymnasium was the perfect trap for us. Their wrestling coach had recruited many Mergenthaler High School grapplers and Baltimore County champions from the 1970 high school graduation class and quietly won a lot of matches. Now that Baltimore University's wrestling team was academically eligible, they instantly became a major force in the Mason Dixon Conference.

As the match proceeded our lightweights did reasonably well, until the match reached the 158 pound weight class. Their 158 pound wrestler, who was the 1970 MSA wrestling champion from Mervo Tech, crushed our wrestler, who was good. Then my match began at the 167 pound weight class and I lost a one point decision. When our co-captain lost to their 1970 Baltimore County champion at the 177 pound weight class, the match was nearly lost. But our 190 pound wrestler pinned his opponent and Towson State led by one point. But our heavyweight who was grossly outweighed, got pinned and Baltimore University won the match. With this victory Baltimore University secured the Mason Dixon Conference dual meet trophy.

In a state of shock, the Tigers went to Glassboro State College(now Rowan College) in New Jersey and lost again. I tied my opponent, which did not help our cause. After this match the wrestling team had a closed door meeting. One of the results of the meeting was that I wrestled at the 177 pound weight class. Our one co-captain wrestled at the 167 pound weight class and the other at 150 pounds. Both were awesome senior wrestlers. The following week, we defeated Western Maryland College and Millersville State College of Pennsylvania. I defeated my Western Maryland opponent but lost to Millersville. For the year my overall record was five wins two losses and a tie. But Towson State had an eleven win and three loss record before the Mason Dixon Conference Wrestling Tournament and was hungry for a conference trophy.

The 1972 Mason Dixon Conference Wrestling Tournament was held at Western Maryland College. After the seeding meeting of all the wrestlers in the tournament ended, our coach and co-captains held a closed door session with all ten starting wrestlers. Basically what was said was that the ten best wrestlers of the entire conference were sitting in that motel room. I liked the idea and so did everyone else. Of all the pep talks that I've ever heard, this one was the best of all the rest. Now all our team had to do was wrestle well.

That night on the mats of our bitter rivals, Towson State's wrestling team found a new friend by the name of momentum. We won every match but two, and sent eight of our ten starters to the conference championship finals. Even the two losses were noteworthy. Our 142 pound wrestler, a freshman from Franklin High School, lost a tough match to his Baltimore University foe who was named as the Mason Dixon Conference's Most Valuable Wrestler. I represented Towson State at the 177 pound weight class and faced the hometown favorite and the defending Mason Dixon Conference 177 pound champion from Western Maryland College. We had some familiarity with each other, as we wrestled each other at the South Atlantic AAU Tournament in 1971. Encouraged by the vociferous crowd, the six foot four inch tall champion struggled with the five foot eight inch tall challenger in the semi-finals. As the third period began, the score remained tied until a two point reversal and riding time point earned the champion a close decision. It was the closest margin of victory for this particular champion during his three year reign.

As the Towson State wrestling team took to the mats at Western Maryland College the following day, a thunderous standing ovation erupted from the crowd, as we had already clinched the Mason Dixon Conference Wrestling Tournament trophy. It was one of the proudest moments of my life. I was just glad to be a part of the best group of athletes that I have ever known. But the team still had ten matches to wrestle.

In the consolation finals with a bronze medal for the winner, our freshman 142 pound wrestler from Franklin High School won a hard fought referee's decision over his Western Maryland foe. I lost a one point decision to Loyola College's strong man. The championship finals were wrestled in the same general pattern as the consolation finals. We won four matches and lost four.

Our freshman 118 pound wrestler from Patapsco High School easily defeated his Loyola College opponent. After that match, we lost four championship finals in a row. Our freshman 126 pound grappler from Bel Air High School lost a close match to Western Maryland. Our junior 134 pound wrestler from Dundalk High School lost a one point decision to Loyola College's captain and 1969 MSA champion from Archbishop Curley High School. Our senior co-captain at 150 pounds from Mount Saint Joseph High School lost a two point decision to Hampden Sydney College's super freshman, who was Virginia state high school wrestling champion. Our junior 158 pound wrestler from Prince George's County again got demolished by Baltimore University's second best wrestler and 1970 MSA wrestling champion. Our other senior co-captain at the 167 pound weight class pinned Hampden Sydney's other fearless freshman in the first period to atone for the other co-captain's loss. Our senior 190 pound wrestler from Dundalk High School easily pinned his opponent from Washington College. Our senior 210 pound heavyweight from Baltimore Polytechnic Institute finished the finals with a victory over his heavier rival from Western Maryland. I admired our heavyweight because he was always lighter than his opponents and still managed to win most of his matches.

Upon completion of the tournament, Towson State College finished in first, followed by Baltimore University, host Western Maryland College and then Loyola College. The rest of the schools finished with fewer points. I still remember the picture of our team holding the Mason Dixon Conference trophy as wrestling champions. I wrestled on a championship team and finished with a winning record for the season.

When my parents awakened me that Sunday morning, dad beamed from ear to ear. He was finally proud of me. However the *Baltimore Sunpapers* listed my name as Mike Harrison in the consolation finals. Sometimes the media errs, but they got the score right and that is all that really mattered. I actually looked forward to attending church and thanking God for this moment. Towson State still had four champions thanking God too, as their season continued into the following week's Division III National Wrestling Tournament at Oswego State College in New York. All of our wrestlers except our 118 pound wrestler got eliminated in the first round. He advanced to the second round and then got eliminated from the national tournament by a wrestler from Northern Iowa. For all of the wrestling team, it was back to the books.

Being buoyed up by a new spirit of optimism as a result of our successful wrestling season, I studied hard during the spring semester of 1972. I was rewarded with the most successful results in four semesters of college study. I passed sixteen semester hours of course study which is the normal work load per student. Although I only averaged 2.22 or a C+ average for the semester, I was happy with the progress.

Something happened in my neighborhood during this time period which really sweetened the spring.

In April my old newspaper boss attempted to trade his 1963 Pontiac Grand Prix to the automobile dealership for a newer vehicle. The dealer only offered him a small amount for his car and he was visibly upset. He said that if anyone offered him more money, he would sell the vehicle to them immediately. As I had money in savings for the purpose of buying a car, I offered him a dollar more than the dealer had for his car. He accepted my offer and I bought my first vehicle. Now I felt momentum was on my side, but there was a fly in the ointment.

Bethlehem Steel did not have a summer program for college students in 1972 so I had to look for work elsewhere. Alma Harrison came to the rescue as usual. A moving van company that had moved furniture at Fort Holabird told mother that they needed some additional help. As summer is the biggest boon of the year for the moving industry, I applied for a job at this moving van company. Although three dollars an hour wasn't much in earnings, it was better than no earnings. With the extra hours worked, I made up the difference of the hourly wage from Bethlehem Steel. Summer flew by with the daily car drive to work. I made money, dated my girlfriend and had fun.

Also during that summer the Harrison family found a new vacation resort, the Outer Banks of North Carolina. The place that dad thought was heaven on earth was a fishing pier at Rodanthe North Carolina. As Robert graduated from grammar school and Janet was within one year of the same feat, the family went south and thoroughly enjoyed it. The biggest headlines during that summer came from the Watergate office complex in Washington D.C. A bungled burglary attempt on the Democratic party headquarters there became of greater importance as that summer sizzled. But September beckoned and my junior year began at Towson State.

That semester, I took fifteen credit hours which was a normal class load. In an attempt to pass my second English course, which was a requirement to graduate, I encountered a major stumbling block. On the first day of class, the English professor began an outline of requirements to be performed for successful completion of her English class. Term papers had to be completed monthly, six books had to be read, and three examinations had to be passed for a passing grade. When I dropped the course during the first Friday of the fall semester, I realized that half of the class had already done the same thing. But I still carried twelve credits that semester, and three of the remaining four courses were in my major field of study. By this time I worked during the day as a busboy, which made it easier to complete studies at night. But if school was tough, wrestling was worse.

All of out starting team except our returning 126 pound conference finalist, senior 158 pound conference finalist and me, graduated or performed at another sport. With a lack of experience already, Towson State's strength of schedule was dramatically increased. Instead of wrestling the basketball colleges of Washington D.C. in December, we started our schedule with the wrestling powerhouses of Pennsylvania. The results were perfectly predictable. Our first match of the season was a triangular meet against Kutztown State and Shippensburg State Colleges at Shippensburg. Towson State lost to both schools and I lost both of my matches at the 177 pound weight class. For the first time in college, I got pinned by Shippensburg's strong 177 pound wrestler. The following week Towson State hosted Gettysburg College. There were no repercussions from the previous year's riot, but we still lost the match and I did as well. Towson State and I were both winless for the year. I quit the team in disgust. I informed our wrestling coach the following day about my decision and said it was because of final examinations. Coach and I knew better.

I was frustrated in wrestling because I couldn't defeat our freshman 167 pound wrestler in a wrestle-off. He was from Harford County and was a state wrestling finalist from the previous year. I felt that my two years collegiate experience would help me in this situation, but to no avail. He wrestled at the 167 pound weight and I wrestled at the 177 pound weight, even though both were the same height and approximately the same weight. I won challenges against others in the wrestling room, but I wasn't a very good 177 pound wrestler. Most football players shed weight from their normal 190 pounds and above, to participate at the 177 pound weight class during wrestling season. By contrast I weighed one hundred seventy-five pounds during the off season and reduced my weight by ten pounds during wrestling season. As most of my opponents were at least ten pounds heavier than me, it had a telling effect on my matches in the third period. At this point in time I wasn't sure what to do, until my wrestling coach called me at home during final examination week. He said "I need you. Come on back to the team after the first of the year." I needed to hear that from him.

As far as the semester was concerned, I earned two B grades and two C grades for a 2.5 grade point average with twelve earned semester hours. After five semesters of college, I earned sixty-four credits or exactly half the amount of credits needed to graduate. I was one full semester behind my classmates and at that rate, it would take an extra year to obtain a degree after the state scholarship expired. Needless to say there was a lot of work to finish.

As I practiced during the second week of January, most of the other wrestlers were lukewarm toward my readmission to the wrestling team. The two co-captains were dormitory students and so was the rest of the team, except our 134 pound wrestler from Milford Mill High School. The dorm students had their own clique, and they made it plainly obvious that I was not welcome to join. I didn't really care what they wanted. I was in it to win it, or at least get to the conference finals in my weight class. But at this point in time any kind of victory made me happy as I had lost five matches in succession.

My first match in January 1973 was against the University of West Virginia at Morgantown, West Virginia. I got my first win in eleven months, but the Tigers lost to the Mountaineers. Actually I caught a break, in that I defeated their reserve 177 pound wrestler by a major decision. The following week we were in action against two Baltimore rivals. Towson State defeated Loyola College, which was a conference member. I wrestled poorly against Loyola and lost by decision. Our wrestling coach openly questioned my desire to compete in front of my teammates. But I did wrestle better against Morgan State College of the Mideastern Athletic Conference. We defeated the Bears by a solitary point and I tied my opponent. My opponent from Morgan State was the 1971 MSA wrestling champion from Southern High School. He normally wrestled at the 158 pound weight class and attempted to lose weight to reach the 150 pound weight class. With his speed he grabbed an early lead and then I emerged from my funk. In the third period with the weight advantage in my favor, I scored four straight points, and nearly turned my opponent onto his back at the buzzer. Nevertheless some in the dormitory clique were not satisfied with the effort, and made their feelings known to the wrestling coach. Our coach started another wrestler at my weight class in the team's next match at Western Maryland College. I stayed home and Towson State lost the match.

Our wrestling coach called me into his office the next day and apologized to me. I accepted his apology and looked forward to wrestling our next home match against Johns Hopkins University. Towson State prevailed over Johns Hopkins and I defeated their 177 pound wrestler on my twenty-first birthday. I stopped by the Brentwood Inn that night and had my first legal drink with friends. As I sobered up that Sunday, I realized that the spring semester began the following day.

When the spring semester started that Monday, I was more determined to do well in college. I needed good grades and many credits in the worst way. But there was less than three weeks left in wrestling season and I was determined to change my losing ways.

Our first match of the semester was against Millersville State in Pennsylvania. Towson State and I lost a very close match. The following Saturday was a home match against our main conference nemesis, the Baltimore University Bees. Baltimore University defeated us and earned their second consecutive Mason Dixon Conference dual meet trophy. I lost to their 177 pound wrestler, a 1970 Baltimore County champion from Overlea High School. I gave it a good effort, but caught some bad breaks. Even my opponent said "You are the first wrestler that I've ever wrestled, who had a stalling point called against him while attempting a takedown." But that was only one point of the nine points that he scored against me. Our final match of the season was against Glassboro State College of New Jersey at home. With a losing season insured, this was the wrestling team's last chance to show off its muscle during the regular season.

On that day we resembled the previous year's team. Our lightweights demolished Glassboro State's lightweights and the match was almost over by the time of my 167 pound match. I wrestled the defending NAIA national champion, who was an undefeated senior with fifteen straight pins. My opponent was five foot six inches tall and had as many muscles as *The Hulk*. When I took my opponent down with a double leg takedown, Towson State's fans erupted in jubilation. The joy was short lived as my foe quickly tied the match, and held a precarious two point lead, heading into the final period of the match. He forced me onto my back to win by decision, but without a pin. My opponent was so upset that one would have thought that he had lost the match. He kept shouting "I'll see you in the nationals." I didn't have the courage to tell him that his college was in the NAIA, not Towson State's division. The NAIA is a national group of colleges with the smallest enrollment of students. Nevertheless Glassboro State's 167 pound wrestler won his second consecutive NAIA championship in 1973. However, Towson State won its final dual meet of the regular season at home. Now it was preparation time for the Mason Dixon Conference Wrestling Tournament. We did not have far to travel as we were the host school in 1973.

Baltimore University was a huge favorite in this tournament and did not disappoint their following. Towson State's best chances for conference champions were our co-captains at 126 pounds and 158 pounds and our two new freshmen stars, at the 150 and 177 pound weight classes. I wrestled at the 167 pound weight class in this tournament, which was my normal weight class.

All four of our best wrestlers advanced to the conference finals. Our 126 pound wrestler from Bel Air High won his first Mason Dixon Conference championship. Our senior co-captain from Prince George's County also won a conference championship as well. Our two new 'super freshmen' lost in the conference finals and earned silver medals. Meanwhile, I had my dream match in the quarterfinals against Baltimore University's best wrestler. He took a two point margin into the final period of our match and pulled away for the decision. It was the last time that he wrestled a full eight minute match in this tournament. Having won only two matches and a tie all year, I won two consolation matches that Saturday and earned a bronze medal for third place in my weight class. Towson State College also took third place in this tournament, just two points behind second place Western Maryland College. I finished the season with a losing record for the first time in my career. I was disappointed in the entire season as a whole, but felt that I had improved my skills by the season's conclusion. I was a work in progress and progress was what I needed in my spring semester classes.

Just as in the previous semester of my junior year, I dropped one course and passed four other courses. As in the previous semester, I earned B grades in two courses and C grades in the other two courses. With the additional twelve credits earned that semester I now totaled seventy-six credits earned in college. That total was fifty-two credits short of graduation. By this time, I began thinking that I would not graduate in 1974, even by the end of the year. I needed a summer break badly to change my pessimistic outlook in the year 1973.

CHAPTER V

SENIOR CHAMPIONSHIP YEAR OF 1974

B y the summer of 1973 I became painfully aware that time was running out for me to successfully earn a college degree. For the next eighteen months I had a sense of urgency about everything necessary to reach my goals. Due to uncle Sam's influence again, Bethlehem Steel hired me that summer for a good wage. In the *Continuing College Student Program*, I worked in the rod and wire mill every week until September. Also that summer President Nixon, our commander-in-chief, negotiated a peace settlement with North Vietnam and began recalling troops back home. It was one of his 1972 campaign promises and temporarily diverted news from the infamous *Watergate Scandal*, as it was referred to by then. With the presidential administration in chaos, I worked with new financial obligations.

My initial automobile began having a serious valve tapping problem. With all of the maintenance that I had already provided for the vehicle, more expensive issues lurked on the horizon. In the midst of this personal crisis dad came to the rescue. As dad had purchased several cars in his lifetime from used car salesmen, he took me on a tour of used car lots.

With dad's encouragement, I bought a 1967 Pontiac Lemans and enjoyed it immensely for the next few years. I now had a reliable vehicle for the remaining days in college, although with eighteen payments. The Harrison family without me ventured to Nags Head, North Carolina for a week, while I entertained my girlfriend at home. Nevertheless I was good while they were gone, working hard daily at Bethlehem Steel. As August faded, September beckoned, and senior year began.

With a renewed sense of urgency, I took fifteen credits that semester with one major difference from the past. I had to pass all five courses or I would be ineligible to student teach during the spring semester. For one to student teach at Towson State, one had to be a senior in class standing, which meant having earned at least ninety semester hours. With the completion of fifteen credit hours, I would accumulate ninety-one credit hours by spring semester. My back was to the mat and I knew it. But that is when champions usually perform at their best. I worked at the Brentwood Inn that semester as a bartender's assistant. I mixed drinks, filled drink orders, stocked beer, and washed drink glasses. Without temporary employment at the Brentwood Inn, I would have never remained financially viable in college. If there was a real sense of urgency about studies, there was an even greater sense of purpose for the upcoming wrestling season.

By October 1973 I lifted a lot of weight. I worked out so hard that year, that I bench-pressed two hundred seventy-five pounds, even though I weighed about a hundred pounds less than that weight. The previous year I had bench pressed two hundred fifty pounds on the efficient *Nautilus* machine at Towson State. But I was stronger than ever, or at least twenty-five pounds stronger than junior year. This was my last chance to live out my dream from the 1964 MSA Finals on television. I knew before wrestling season began the identity of the black, undefeated wrestling champion. That was Baltimore University's 167 pound two-time undefeated Mason Dixon Conference wrestling champion. The only question that remained that year was the identity of his opposition in the conference finals. As wrestling practice progressed in November, I received an awesome invitation from Archbishop Curley High School.

The varsity football team had an undefeated season, and invited all Curley alumni to attend the final game of the season against Cardinal Gibbons at home. While the priests and lay teachers provided the refreshments, it was difficult for anyone to refuse a deal like that. Some Dundalk friends and I watched Curley dismantle Gibbons for a perfect football season. I drank beer before and during the game, ate a lot of cold cuts in the cafeteria after the game, and thoroughly enjoyed the whole experience. I needed this day to take a break from reality. This Curley football team did something in one day that we could not do in my four years, which was to defeat Cardinal Gibbons. If Saturday was a great day for high school football in November, Monday was a somber day for college wrestling practice.

That day it was announced that we would wrestle the University of Maryland at College Park in a preseason wrestling scrimmage on a week day after Thanksgiving. Maryland had a great wrestling program and dominated the Atlantic Coast Conference, winning twenty of twenty-one conference wrestling tournaments between the years 1959 and 1980. As this preseason match fell into that time span, our wrestling team had a daunting task. Despite the awesome ability of our opponent, our starting team only lost this preseason wrestling match by five points to a Division I powerhouse. I actually won a close decision at 167 pounds, the weight class at which I wrestled most of the year. As the previous year's freshman sensation had dropped out of school, it was my weight class by default. It did not matter as long as the match was won. I embraced Oakland Raiders football team owner Al Davis's adage of "Just win baby." Close wins became typical of my wrestling style that year.

Towson State's wrestling program improved somewhat over the previous year as well. Our two co-captains were a junior 126 pound defending Mason Dixon Conference champion from Bel Air High School and a sophomore 158 pound Mason Dixon Conference finalist from Bladensburg High School. Both were passionate wrestlers and served the team well. The question became, how far would the team improve over the previous year's fiasco. One could only hope for improvement with a bunch of sophomores and me. Nevertheless we had nine of ten starters from the previous year on the wrestling team.

Our first match was a triangular meet against Pennsylvania powers Kutztown State and Shippensburg State at home. We were blitzed the previous year by both schools, but improved our performance this time. Actually Towson State and Kutztown State both defeated Shippensburg, but two matches determined the outcome of the triangular meet. My match at 167 pounds and our heavyweight's match were all that remained of our match against Kutztown. They enjoyed a three point lead over us, but if both Towson State wrestlers won their matches, we would win the triangular meet.

My Kutztown foe and I had both beaten our Shippensburg opponent earlier, and knew this match would be decisive. With the score tied in the third period and both of us penalized a point for stalling, the referee warned us to wrestle. With forty-five seconds left in the match, I scored a two point takedown and took a two point lead in the match. With thirty seconds left, my opponent scored a one point escape to cut the lead to one point. Afraid to have a stalling point called against me, I tried my best to stave off my opponent and protect the one point lead. Disaster struck with two seconds left in the match. He took me down for two points and the victory. Now with a secure six point lead and one match left, Kutztown State celebrated their tight win and my 'three second meltdown'. Our heavyweight defeated their heavyweight but did not pin him, which would have tied us with Kutztown by virtue of a six point pin. Kutztown State escaped with a win, Towson placed second, and Shippensburg finished last. This "three second meltdown" bothered me the rest of that year. I remembered how painful it felt and never wanted it to happen again.

The following week were two tough matches against Gettysburg College in Pennsylvania and Elizabethtown State of Pennsylvania at home. As a senior, I cautioned our sophomores about the reception we received the last time that Towson ventured to Gettysburg. Our younger guys didn't have a clue, but the Gettysburg crowd had not forgotten us. The crowd was abusive and tried to bait some of our wrestlers into a fistfight. This was Gettysburg's first home match, as they had previously lost a quadrangular meet to three Ivy League schools. As a matter of fact, my opponent at 167 pounds was the only Gettysburg wrestler with an undefeated record against that competition. Towson State lost the match and I dropped a decision against a tough opponent. He eventually lost more weight and placed fifth in the 158 pound weight class at the

Division III National Wrestling Tournament that year. He was an All-American, who were any of the top six finishers in their respective weight classes in the national tournament.

The following match at Towson State was more of the same routine. Towson lost the match to Elizabethtown State and I wrestled their best wrestler at the 177 pound weight class. I lost the match by a respectable margin of five points. This wrestler lost pounds to reach the 167 pound weight class in the Division III National Tournament and placed sixth, earning All-American status. The wrestling team and I had a one win and three loss record. We both needed a win badly on the last week before final examinations. Towson State faced University of Maryland at Baltimore County at their campus and Loyola College at home. Both schools were in the Mason Dixon Conference.

Our wrestlers ventured to U.M.B.C. on a Tuesday night and marveled at their facilities. Their gymnasium was awesome, but we had a singular purpose for our visit. Towson State had never lost to the Retrievers in wrestling and I faced their 167 pound Mason Dixon Conference finalist from the previous year. Knowing that this was a key match to a successful season, I took a three point lead after the first period with two takedowns. Even though I was penalized a stalling point, I still won the match and started my senior year with a solid conference win.

Our next match was against Loyola College and proved to be our easiest test of the year. As the Greyhounds had only four wrestlers available they forfeited the match, as they had lost a majority of the wrestled matches. By Christmas break, Towson State had a perfect conference record. My overall record was two wins and three losses. At this point in the season, I was three seconds from a winning record. Although content about the improvement over the previous year's wrestling record, I was elated about my grades that semester.

The fall semester of 1973 was my best semester of academic achievement at Towson State College. Needing fifteen credits to become a senior and thus be eligible to student teach the following semester, I passed all five of my courses that semester. I earned four B grades and one C grade for a 2.8 grade point average or a solid B- average. My overall GPA now reached a respectable 2.39 with ninety-one semester credits passed. Everything started to click for me as the year 1974 began.

I always felt that the year 1974 could become the best year of my life. In many ways because of my previous announced goals for college, wrestling, and work, it came true. But as is true with many years in one's life, that year wasn't perfect. But as far as I was concerned, that year was the best. The wrestling team started 1974 in mid-January with a triangular meet at home against West Virginia University and Morgan State College. Our wrestling team defeated the Bears of Morgan State but lost to the Mountaineers of West Virginia. For the second time that year, we took second place in a triangular meet at home. I defeated a freshman who was West Virginia state champion in high school by a close decision. However in the last match of the triangular meet, I lost to Morgan State's stellar 167 pound wrestler by a close decision. He won the Mid Eastern Athletic Conference, which was a conference of black American institutions of higher learning, located on the east coast. The Morgan State coach told me that "The 167 pound match looked like a conference final." In many ways he was right. I wrestled well but not well enough to win the match. Towson State's next opponent was a new Mason Dixon Conference member.

The Towson State Tigers in our gold wrestling singlets with *TSC* in black letters emblazoned on the chest, traveled to Salisbury Maryland and wrestled Salisbury State College. The Seagulls in their first year in the Mason Dixon Conference, competed for the conference dual meet trophy. Because they were ineligible for the conference tournament trophy, Salisbury State did not compete in the wrestling tournament that year. Towson State defeated Salisbury, but I faced the best wrestler on the opposing team as usual. He had lost just one match against Baltimore University, and had a phenomenal record. In front of their home crowd, I took a three point lead into the final period of the match. But I had the flu that week and ran out of steam. He rallied to tie the match and took a one point lead with thirty seconds left in the match, when I was penalized a point for stalling. I tried to score in vain, but my opponent stopped all of my moves. Because I was awarded one point for riding time during the match, the match ended in a tie. But Towson State was undefeated in the Mason Dixon Conference and I was as well.

Our next two opponents during the last week before spring semester, were Western Maryland and Johns Hopkins. The Towson State Tigers continued our winning ways at home by defeating Western Maryland College. I won a thriller at 167 pounds against another tough freshman, who had won the Delaware high school state championship. I won a decision by a single point, despite yielding two stalling points to my opponent. Our wrestling team then visited Johns Hopkins University. In three years of wrestling against them, this was our closest margin of victory, as we won by just ten points. I won my final match against Johns Hopkins by a decision to conclude an undefeated record against them. Towson State was undefeated in the conference and had an overall record of six wins and four losses. Baltimore University was the only obstacle between us and a Mason Dixon Conference dual meet trophy. With three weeks left in wrestling, I had a winning record at the outset of February. I had more wins already than the previous year without any conference losses.

But spring semester started that Monday and just five weeks from that date, I would student teach somewhere. Everything was happening quickly and I needed to accept the challenge. After Monday's classes started, the wrestling team had a tough challenge against Millersville State College at home. Unfortunately for us, Millersville State demolished Towson State in wrestling. As in most of my matches that year, I wrestled their best wrestler at the 177 pound weight class. The previous year I had lost to this opponent by a narrow decision in Pennsylvania, but his skills had improved dramatically. At six foot three inches tall, he scored four takedowns and embarrassed me by a major decision in the last home match of my career. My opponent from Millersville remained at the 177 pound weight class and placed sixth in the Division III National Tournament at this weight class. Again I lost to another All-American. Towson State's overall record dropped to six wins and five losses, and completed our home schedule. My overall record also regressed at this time. But my ego suffered another embarrassing blow during that particular week.

For the first time in two years, I lost a wrestle-off in practice to another teammate. He was a judo expert and I fell for his favorite move. My teammate started against Glassboro State of New Jersey and then Baltimore University. Towson State defeated Glassboro State but lost the Mason Dixon Conference dual met trophy to Baltimore University. Their 167 pound defending conference champion pinned my replacement, but he pinned everyone during that particular year. I was the last conference wrestler to finish an eight minute match with Baltimore University's best wrestler, and that was in the quarterfinals of the 1973 Mason Dixon Conference wrestling tournament. But I wasn't even a starter for Towson State with two weeks left in the season.

During the following week, I challenged my teammate and got one last chance at redemption. In the presence of the wrestling team, I defeated my teammate in a wrestle-off and regained the starting position at 167 pounds. My back was to the mat and I delivered, as there was no tomorrow. Our last match was a triangular meet at York College in Pennsylvania, where Towson State faced York College and Lincoln Tech. Towson State lost to York College miserably and then demolished Lincoln Tech. I faced York's best wrestler with an undefeated record at the 167 pound weight class.

My opponent was six foot tall and not that muscular. However he was the fastest wrestler that I had ever wrestled, and he pinned me in the second period of the match, after I slammed him onto the mat. This was only the second time that I had been pinned in my collegiate career. My overall record plummeted as a result of this season ending loss. But my opponent from York College remained undefeated for the entire season and won the Division III National Wrestling Tournament at the 167 pound weight class. Needless to say, he was the best wrestler that I faced in 1974. Our wrestling coach allowed my teammate to wrestle against Lincoln Tech and he got an easy pin. Although I could have used a win, I waited until the following week in the conference tournament. Towson State finished the season with an overall winning record and just one conference loss. The question became, was this team improved enough to win the conference tournament? Just like everything else in life, time would tell the story.

The thirtieth annual Mason Dixon Conference Tournament in 1974 was held at Gallaudet College in Washington D.C. Gallaudet was the nationally renowned college for the hearing impaired and had fine facilities for a conference wrestling tournament. Baltimore University with all of their returning conference champions, was an overwhelming favorite to win the tournament. Their wrestling team had even tied Maryland, the Atlantic Coast Conference champion, in a dual meet during that season. So their team was ready to defend the conference tournament trophy and all of their wrestlers were healthy.

Towson State's health issues surfaced, when it was discovered that our 126 pound co-captain and defending conference champion had suffered a season ending injury. Now Towson State was really behind the proverbial eight ball. After the seeding meeting of all wrestling coaches that Friday another issue arose. After our coach distributed the seeding chart to each individual, I threw my paperwork at the floor in disgust. When our coach asked what was wrong, I told him that the coaches had seeded me fourth in my weight class behind the second seeded U.M.B.C. wrestler, whom I had defeated during the regular season. I also informed our coach that I had not lost to any of the wrestlers in that weight class during the season. He took my paperwork back to the seeding committee and the wrestling coaches changed me to the third seed in that weight class, with U.M.B.C.'s wrestler still seeded second. The committee's thinking was logical. The wrestler from U.M.B.C. and I should wrestle each other in the semi-finals to settle the seeding issue. Our coach then told me "You better make this work." I nodded and said "I will coach." He then remarked "You have the worst undefeated conference record that I've ever seen." Receiving sixteen stalling points against me in twelve matches that year, I understood his logic. But then I muttered "just win baby" and prepared for my upcoming match.

With the tournament starting that Friday, Baltimore University assumed an early lead. With our 126 pound wrestler out of action, our heavier weights assumed the daunting task of trying to keep up with Baltimore University. Our other co-captain, a sophomore and top seed at 158 pounds from Bladensburg High School, easily advanced to the conference finals. Towson State's 177 pound wrestler, a junior from Oxon Hill, advanced to the conference finals. Our 190 pound class wrestler, a sophomore from Paint Branch High School, wrestled well that Friday and also advanced to the conference finals. Our sophomore heavyweight wrestler from John Carroll High added to our list of finalists in the tournament. All three of our heaviest wrestlers played for the football team and were truly great athletes. Now it was my turn at the 167 pound weight class to complete the list of Towson State finalists that year.

In the quarterfinals I wrestled Loyola College's best wrestler that year, who was a fourth place finisher in the 1971 MSA Wrestling Tournament. This match remained a tie until the final period, when I got a two point reversal and riding time point for the win. In the semi-finals, I faced Western Maryland College's super freshman and former Delaware state champion, who upset U.M.B.C.'s second seeded wrestler. As I had only defeated him by a point during the regular season, one expected a close match, and it lived up to its expectations. My opponent secured a two point takedown in the opening period and held that slim lead until the second period. Then our coach yelled at me "You keep turning one way." He was right as I kept using my outside switch move and my opponent kept stopping it. I reverted to the inside switch move and immediately got an escape point. Losing by one point and with a championship berth on the line, I scored a double leg takedown against my Western Maryland foe for the lead. Then I controlled my opponent for the rest of the match, earning a riding time point and the decision. I went to the championship finals and wrestled the best wrestler in the Mason Dixon Conference in Washington D.C. My dream was fulfilled ten years after viewing the 1964 MSA championship finals on television.

Entering the final day of competition, Towson State had every wrestler eligible to be a conference champion from the 158 pound weight class and above. We were only twelve points behind first place Baltimore University before Saturday's championship finals. We had to win all five of our matches to surpass Baltimore University and win the Mason Dixon Conference wrestling tournament. In three of those final matches Towson State faced a Baltimore University wrestler. Because we had five wrestlers in consecutive weight classes in the conference finals, the group became collectively known as *The Five*. But all five wrestlers had to win to steal Baltimore University's thunder.

The morning of February 23rd was clear and cold in Washington D.C. Our wrestling team had breakfast and I realized that this was the last time that I would ever enjoy the company of this group. This was truly a fantastic moment.

The Five were still alive and we were all ready to take our last shot at glory. By the time the 158 pound match began which represented Towson State's first finalist, Western Maryland was in second place by two points over us. This was due to the fact that Western Maryland College had produced four consolation champions, and added a lot of points to their total. At the same time Towson State had only produced two bronze medalists at the 126 and 134 pound weight classes in the consolation finals. At the 158 pound weight class, our wrestler from Bladensburg High School and former Maryland state wrestling champion, defeated his Baltimore University foe by decision and cut Baltimore University's lead to a mere nine points with four matches left. Towson State had surpassed Western Maryland College again into second place. Now the championship finals proceeded to the 167 pound weight class.

One of the referees at the tournament joked with me that day saying "You're up against a mountain and you basically have no chance of winning the championship." I told him "Someone's got to wrestle the champion and it might as well be me." The referee had a point, in that I had outscored all of my conference opponents by a mere eleven points in six matches without a defeat, including the tournament. But our wrestling coach told me "If you win this match, even if it is by one point, I'll vote for you for conference most valuable wrestler." I needed the encouragement from my coach and an additional incentive to win.

For Towson State to win the tournament trophy, I needed to win and became very aggressive in the match. In the first period, I shot takedowns without any success against my Baltimore University foe. Eventually he secured a takedown for an early lead before the second period. This early lead didn't deter me, as I expected it from him. As I had choice of top or bottom referee's position in the second period, I chose the top position. Knowing that my opponent and I were approximately the same strength, even though he was taller than me, I hoped to wear his body down with my weight and muscle. With my opponent's advantage in moves and speed, this was my best chance to win the championship. For about a minute my plan worked to perfection.

I stopped all of his moves and when we went off the mat, my teammates clapped and shouted their approval. But my opponent was getting frustrated, as no other wrestler in this conference had ever controlled him for that length of time. He then stood up and I reached across his body to control his leg. With my body temporarily off balance, he slammed my body hard into the mat and compressed all of his weight upon my chest. It was such a stunning maneuver, that I was caught off balance and gasped for air. When I heard the slap of the referee's palm on the mat, I knew the match and my wrestling career had ended. This opponent was the last conference wrestler to defeat me, exactly one year before this match. Since that loss, I had seven wins and a tie in the conference. Meanwhile my Baltimore University opponent was proclaimed the Mason Dixon Conference Most Valuable Wrestler by unanimous vote.

The importance of that match was that Baltimore University had clinched their second consecutive conference tournament trophy. However three individual matches remained and second place in the conference tournament was still undecided. Our junior 177 pound wrestler from Oxon Hill Maryland, endured a tough two point loss in the finals to the best wrestler from George Mason University of Virginia. Our sophomore 190 pound wrestler from Paint Branch High School lost a heartbreaker to the other senior Baltimore University defending conference champion. Our sophomore heavyweight from John Carroll High School completed the onslaught by losing a last second decision to Western Maryland College's heavyweight. This final match insured Western Maryland College of a second place finish and relegated Towson State to third. The tournament was mercifully over and we had only one conference champion.

During the first week of March 1974, the Division III National Wrestling Tournament was held in Long Beach, California, where all wrestlers had hoped to end their respective seasons. Only one Towson State wrestler attended and that was our 158 pound conference champion. He actually won one match, giving Towson State a point total in the national wrestling tournament. But the big winner in the nationals in 1974 was the conference's most valuable wrestler from Baltimore University. He won three matches at the 167 pound weight class and nearly a fourth, when he lost a heartbreaking decision in the national tournament to his opponent from Wisconsin-Green Bay, who placed fifth or All-American.

All totaled that year, I lost four matches to All-American wrestlers, one match to a near All-American, and one match to a conference champion who wrestled in the national tournament. With six of my seven losses to wrestlers in the Division III National Wrestling Tournament, my lone bad loss was the "three second meltdown" in the initial triangular meet of the year. After observing all of the wrestlers that I had lost to during the season on the national tournament's medals podium, our wrestling coach supposedly quipped "I have renewed respect for Chris Harrison." Although my senior record yielded just seven wins seven losses and a tie, I faced an extremely difficult schedule that year. I improved dramatically over the previous year's performance and wrestled for a championship. After all that transpired in wrestling season, I was glad to begin student teaching in March.

I reported to nearby Dundalk High School on that date and met the classroom instructor, whose classes I assisted in teaching for ten weeks that semester. In addition to this course, I took a one credit course on Introduction to Audio Visual Aides, which taught prospective teacher candidates how to operate a movie projector, filmstrip projector, and overhead projector in a classroom setting. Finally I took a three credit course on Teaching Reading in the Secondary School. Upon completion of that course, I realized the importance of reading to a successful classroom environment. But my focus of study was the ten credit course in Student Teaching. As this was a pass/fail course, one did not receive a letter grade. I knew what I wanted but it was difficult to pass the course.

The cooperating teacher was a very knowledgeable and easygoing lady who had taught at Dundalk High School for many years. She showed me the ropes and answered my exasperating questions about teaching. On the second Friday of my student teaching semester, her homeroom and the rest of the student body at Dundalk took a field trip to New York City. It was exciting to see the *Empire State Building*, the *Statue of Liberty* from the Staten Island ferry, and *Radio City Music Hall*. But the best experience that I had in New York was eating dinner at *Mama Leone's Restaurant*. By the third week of student teaching, I taught most of the cooperating teacher's classes. Then I nearly committed a fatal error while teaching history class.

My cooperating teacher gave me a stern look of disapproval and slammed the classroom door after I went on a political diatribe against the Republican Party. In fact she cautioned against political ranting of any sort in her classes or one would fail the student teaching course. The teacher told me when discussing politics, to present the facts about both political parties. She then said that the students should decide which political party they liked and why they liked that party. She also said that one should not interject an opinion unless a student requested it. I wish the mainstream media of today had learned this valuable lesson about American politics. As a matter of interest, I student taught two tenth grade college prep classes World History, and three eleventh grade general studies students, American History. The tenth graders who were classmates of my brother Robert, were a joy to teach and a high level of enthusiasm for World History. Their eleventh grade counterparts were anything but enthusiastic about American History.

I passed student teaching on May 24th and celebrated at Ocean City with Robert and his girlfriend Laura who eventually became his wife. I had amassed one hundred and five credits now, but still needed twenty-three credits to graduate. I passed two summer school courses and earned six more credits. While I prepared for summer school and another job, I saw in the local newspaper that Towson State's lacrosse team won the Division II National Championship by defeating Hobart College. Towson State had now won it's first national championship. Now I had another reason to celebrate that summer.

During my last summer in college, I worked at Bethlehem Steel. With wages at five dollars an hour, I had many bills to pay and my uncle Sam to thank for continuous employment there. As I planned to graduate in December 1974, I took Basic Statistics for a letter grade and American Literature on a pass/fail basis. By passing a required English course in this manner, it did not adversely affect my grade point average. For that reason I viewed American Literature as the last obstacle to a bachelor degree in social science. I had discovered the fairest English professor in that department at Towson State and enrolled in his course during that summer. With two books to be read, two examinations to be passed and a term paper to be satisfactorily submitted, it was a fair amount of work for a college English course.

While the two courses of study were pursued, I maintained forty hours of employment all summer at the pipe mill on a rotating shift basis. I worked daylight hours one week, midnight hours the next, and the afternoon shift the following week. I needed the money badly as I needed to pay tuition for the summer courses in June, and fall semester by September. In addition to all of these expenses, I needed money for textbooks also. Finally I needed to pay the balance owed on the Pontiac Lemans.

The biggest event during that summer was not my financial woes, but the resignation of President Richard Nixon in August 1974. With the *Watergate Scandal* a daily news item, and the president's impeachment looming, Richard Nixon resigned the office of the presidency. He now joined his former Vice-President Spiro Agnew as the first to resign their respective offices in American history. Agnew, the former governor of Maryland resigned his office in October 1973. Interim vice-president Gerald Ford became the new president of the United States.

With Washington D.C. embroiled in resignations and scandal, I received a B grade in Basic Statistics and had a B grade in American Literature when the English professor approached me during class. He asked me "Why did you take this course pass/fail, when you've got the third highest grade in the class?" Then I failed the final examination, but still passed the course. I suppose the professor discovered why I took the course on a pass/fail basis. I was pleased to pass my final English course. By Labor Day, I finished my summer job and rested for a few days. I had some money left in the savings account and was ready to register for fall courses. After paying for all of the required textbooks, my account balance dropped to less than one hundred dollars. So I returned to the Brentwood Inn for fall employment. With part-time employment available again, I renewed my final quest for a degree.

During that fall, I took courses that were interesting such as Canadian History, European Geography, and The History of Modern Germany. I took a two credit course on a pass/fail basis, that was intended for elementary education students. The instructor of the course wasn't happy about my inclusion in this class, as I was a secondary education teaching candidate. But I took seventeen semester hours that fall and had my sights set firmly on my goal in December. While attending school that fall, some interesting events occurred in my life.

Towson State's Division III football team had an undefeated record that fall and didn't even merit a playoff berth that year. Some of my former wrestling teammates played on that unbeaten football team. Meanwhile cousin Mark Mrofki, an Archbishop Curley High School graduate, got married that December to a lovely lady named Nancy. His mother, my mother's sister Margaret lived on Broening Highway in

Baltimore for many years and still lives today in Maryland. Mark and Nancy continued their wonderful marriage for many years and it is still going strong. The lovely couple produced two children whom eventually graduated from college. Mark and Nancy Mrofki had a beautiful December wedding and have had a fruitful marriage. Without a steady relationship then, I was just pleased to graduate from college and be the first in my immediate family to do so.

I expedited all of my term papers that semester and prepared for five final examinations in six courses. My European Geography professor exempted any student from the final examination who had an A or B grade and was scheduled to graduate that semester. As my numerical grade average on two examinations in that class was eighty-one percent, I was exempt from the final examination by one point. But I passed all of the other final examinations during three sleepless nights. Soon I was rewarded for four and one half years of steadfast college study. On my final college report card I earned an A grade, four B grades and a passing grade in the two credit course. The seventeen course hours passed and cumulative 3.2 grade point average for the semester, were the best academic results that I had ever attained in college. My total grade point average for four and one half years was a 2.5 GPA or a B- average. When I received my bachelor degree on December 30th, the celebration was complete. The Brentwood Inn donated one bottle of wine, one fifth of Bacardi Rum, and a case of Michelob Beer. I began celebrating that day and did not stop for a while. The special year of 1974 went out in style.

CHAPTER VI

TEACHING SCHOOL AND SERVING IN THE U.S. ARMY IN GERMANY

As the wintry winds blew in January 1975, mother awakened me about 6 A.M. around the tenth of the month. She told me to get dressed and get a job. I told her that I had worked at the Brentwood Inn until 11 P.M. the previous evening. She gave me some good advice saying "Take that new degree that you have been talking about for weeks and use it." As usual mom was right. The last three weeks of January, I applied for teaching positions in the Baltimore City public schools system and the Baltimore parochial schools system. Even though I lived in Baltimore County, I felt there was no chance of obtaining employment there, as most teachers did not quit their jobs until retirement.

As the month of February began and I aimlessly waited for a telephone call to report to work, I noticed in the *Baltimore Sunpapers* that Towson State's wrestling team had performed well that year. On the last weekend of February, I and some friends ventured to George Mason University and watched the Mason Dixon Conference Wrestling Tournament at Fairfax,

Virginia. Towson State easily won the conference tournament trophy in 1975 and I was happy for my former teammates. I thought about some of the harsh lessons that this group had experienced during the last few years and how they had united as a team against adversity. I was proud of my former teammates, shook all of their hands, and waited for a job.

With March's inception, the winds of change directly affected me. I received two telephone calls within the same day about teaching school. One telephone call was from the Maryland State Correctional System about teaching prisoners at the state penitentiary. The other telephone call was from Baltimore City Public Schools wanting me to teach at a junior high school. The main reason that I selected the city public school teaching position was that they had comprehensive health insurance. By the middle of March 1975, I was teaching Social Studies to eighth graders at Clifton Park Junior High School, an inner city institution with a large percentage of black students. I was pleased to begin a teaching career. I had a homeroom full of students, taught four classes, and served as cafeteria monitor. That was good responsibility for an annual salary of nine thousand dollars. At this time I still lived at home with my parents, but that situation changed quickly.

By the third week of April I moved into my own apartment near Herring Run Park, named *Parkside Gardens*. I lived on the third floor and liked the privacy. But the apartment was cockroach infested and had a neighbor who blasted the stereo all night. Thanks to Aunt Margaret, I had furniture and a television to fill in the empty spaces of the apartment. I felt successful at twenty-three years of age. The only negative aspect of my life was that my old girlfriend and I broke up, as she found a new boyfriend. It did not matter as I was never in love with her anyway.

But in April 1975 Clifton Park Junior High School had some serious personal issues of their own, including the busing of students. While *Jackie Blue* was blaring away on the radio, the school administration was trying to uncover ways to bus black students into white neighborhoods and transport more white students to Clifton Park. At the time, there was a total of seven white students in a population of over a thousand students there. The school administration had also heard rumors that some of the newer teachers without tenure could be relegated to other schools or axed from the system. Tenure occurs when a teacher completes three years of teaching in the same school system. It is a form of probation completion in school systems. Knowing that this tumultuous situation could adversely affect me, I looked for employment elsewhere. One certainly wanted to set one's feet on solid ground.

When the Baltimore parochial schools system telephoned me in May, I went for a job interview and successfully obtained the available position. I taught American History at Bishop John Neumann Middle School in east Baltimore in September 1975. The school was actually Saint Brigid's School and included sixth, seventh, and eighth graders from not only that school, but Sacred Heart of Jesus School as well. Even though the salary was less than the public school position, it was truly what I desired at the time.

On May 21, 1975, I received shocking news from my dad. Grandfather Harrison had died of a massive heart attack at sixty-eight years of age. He was playing golf the previous day with a partner at Druid Hill Park. When his partner arrived at my grandfather's car after being delayed five minutes, the golf clubs were scattered and my grandfather lay dying near the trunk of his car. When the ambulance arrived, he had already died. It was a sudden end to his life after one year of retirement from the warehouse delivery business. But he loved golf and his death was quick and merciful. My grandfather had been an alcoholic, but the last ten years of his life, he was sober and a loyal member of *Alcoholics Anonymous*. I loved him very much and we grew close during his life. The funeral was at Saint Rita's Church and I cried intensely. But the next day I returned to teaching Social Studies in a somber mood. During the following week I received a reasonable facsimile of a bachelor's degree on stage at the Baltimore Civic Center before Memorial Day. But I already missed my grandfather and wished that he could have attended this event.

Despite my grandfather's death during the previous week, my college graduation was a beautiful spectacle for the entire family. All of my aunts and uncles attended as well as grandmother Harrison and grandmother Lapka. I became the first person in my family to receive a college degree and everyone was happy. Mom was proud and even dad was pleased. Later that day I introduced two of my college friends to my parents at Loganview Drive and the three Towson State graduates headed to Ocean City for rest and relaxation. The two friends in question were the former Towson State Student Government Association president and the senior class of 1974 president. Both were my old *English Composition and Conversation* course classmates from freshmen year. The month of May truly finished on a positive note.

As I headed back to Baltimore in June, after frolicking with friends at the beach, I picked up a curvy female hitchhiker in Ocean City. She became my temporary girlfriend and love interest for the next three months. When it came to women, I still didn't have a clue about them and had a difficult time with relationships. I finished my teaching assignment at Clifton Park the third week of June, returned to the Brentwood Inn for a job to pay the rent, and killed cockroaches in the apartment. In my spare time I made love to my new girlfriend that summer. But I looked forward to September and a new teaching assignment.

In late August the faculty of Bishop John Neumann Middle School convened at Saint Brigid's School and we received our assignments for the academic year. I had a sixth grade homeroom, taught three American History classes, two sixth grade Science classes, and one class of Teaching Reading, which was a full day's schedule. It was my first full year of teaching and I was determined to make it work. The principal of our middle school was a strict nun whose faculty included mostly nuns. In addition to the nuns, there were three male lay teachers and one female lay teacher. One of the other male teachers had just received his degree in May, which meant that this was his first teaching assignment. The principal was strict on both of us novice teachers, but she was fair. I had a lot to learn about teaching. During the first three months of the school year I was called to the office several times, but survived the ordeal. Meanwhile my new girlfriend did not survive. She attended a party that had illegal drugs and was incarcerated with the group, for possession of marihuana and attempt to distribute same. She was sentenced to five years in prison. This time I lost my new love interest to the law.

As the year 1976 rolled in, I became a better teacher and my students seemed to adjust to my style as well. Blessed with a good speaking voice, I normally had the full attention of my students especially during American History classes. Also I changed the format of my classes on a daily basis. One day it was a directed reading lesson, the next day it was a filmstrip, and the following day it became a current events discussion. I can honestly say that it was rarely boring in those classes. While this classroom progress occurred, my dad encouraged me to buy another automobile. My 1967 Pontiac Lemans had some serious mileage on it and I traded it for a newer Pontiac. I had two years of payments but other storm clouds gathered on the horizon.

There were two irrefutable facts that precluded me from a lengthy teaching career in social studies. The first fact I discovered during my senior year of college. Some fields of study in college were necessary to fill society's needs, such as engineers, doctors and nurses. Social studies was the most saturated major field of study and required few graduates to meet societal needs. By 1976 I was fortunate to be employed as a teacher. The second irrefutable fact became painfully clear by the spring. The *Baby Boom* supply of students born between 1946 and 1964 ended and the *Vietnam Era* supply of students born in 1965 and after had begun. This irrefutable fact produced a large enrollment decrease in middle schools around the country. Because of this thirty percent decline of students, many aspiring teachers lost their jobs during this difficult transition.

As I observed the end of teaching at Bishop John Neumann Middle School and the eighth grade graduation, I became proud of two irrefutable facts. None of the students that I taught failed a single course. The other undeniable fact was that ninety percent of my reading class students improved by at least one grade level at the end of the academic year. The school provided the facts by administering a reading test to all students in early September of the school year and a follow-up reading examination at the end of May in the same academic year. With a total of thirty students in my reading class, twenty-seven advanced at least one grade level in reading, two students remained at the same grade level and one student's reading level actually dropped two grade levels. Overall I was happy with this development. But the other first-year teacher and I were given notice that our services were no longer needed in the classroom. However each of us received a satisfactory job performance report.

Bidding the Brentwood Inn a tearful goodbye, I went to work for the moving company, where I had previously worked in 1972. At least I knew the moving industry had needs especially during the summer. With uncertain employment my main concern, I returned home to my parents at twenty-four years of age. Apartment living was too expensive at this point in my life. My brother Robert worked as an automobile mechanic, upon graduation from Dundalk High School's vocational program. Robert's plan was to bypass college and make his fortune in an industry that society needed. Of course I had already learned about the needs of society from Economics 101 at Towson State.

That same summer my youngest brother Michael graduated from Saint Rita's School and began ninth grade at Archbishop Curley High School. Eventually he detoured back to Dundalk High after completion of ninth grade at Curley. Michael bragged that he never spent a day in junior school. My sister Janet prepared for her senior year at Dundalk High School. Janet was a two sport athlete at Dundalk and an honor student in the college prep courses there. She performed even better at Dundalk Community College.

In August 1976 my family and I vacationed at the Outer Banks of North Carolina. While there I met a stunning twenty-one year old brunette with short hair, blue eyes, glistening white teeth and a figure that *Playboy magazine* would be proud to display. She had a southern accent and hailed from Colonial Heights, Virginia. I was infatuated with her at first sight. I hoped that she would contact me after I gave her my address. On Labor Day I was the most excited man in Dundalk. She wrote and said that she wanted to see me, and gave me directions to her parents' house. I was elated and anxious to see her again. I thought why would anyone that attractive want to see me. Soon my doubts were erased and we spent two wonderful days kissing, hugging and laughing, but no lovemaking. But I was in love and knew it. I didn't want to return to Baltimore, but someone had to work for a living.

During the following week my new girlfriend wrote and said how much she missed me. Seizing an opportunity to upgrade our relationship, I wrote and told her that I was in love with her. This was the worst thing to write at this stage of our relationship. Eventually she decided never to see me again. I pined away for two months, but eventually lost interest in pursuing a relationship with her.

While I was pining away in early December, Towson State's football team made a national statement on television. The football team advanced to the *Amos Alonzo Stagg Bowl*, which was the Division III National Football Championship. Losing by four touchdowns in the fourth quarter to Saint John's College, Towson State scored four consecutive touchdowns and tied the score with one minute left in regulation. Then

Saint John's College completed a long pass and kicked the dramatic game winning field goal as time expired to win the national championship. This game was the only enjoyment that I had during that fall of 1976. Winter brought more bad news and I felt pinned to the mat.

As the old year ended and 1977 began, my options became more limited. Even the moving company opted for layoffs. Before the company released me, I gave my notice and began substitute teaching in Baltimore City public schools. I began work in January using the split schedule program. The school at which I substituted was Hampstead Hill Junior High School or the old Patterson Park High School. The school had five morning classes from 7:30 A.M. until 12 noon and five afternoon classes from 12:30 P.M. until 5 P.M. If one substituted on both shifts, one made fifty dollars daily. But five consecutive classes was all that I desired to teach. After one week of substitute teaching, I received an opportunity to improve my resume.

The ninth grade World History teacher at Hampstead Hill Junior High requested maternity leave after carrying her baby for over six months. I was invited by the school administration to teach her ninth grade students for the rest of the school year. The school system referred to teachers like me as per-diem substitute teachers. I did not like the salary, but loved the opportunity. I had my own set of rules in addition to the school rules, and printed these rules for all of the students' perusal. Most of the students threw my printed set of rules in the trash, left them on their desks or made paper airplanes out of the material.

On Washington's Birthday I made sixty-six telephone calls to the parents of the students in my classes, for noncompliance with classroom rules. On the following day one could have heard a pin drop in those five classes. I worked by the rules and the students' parents listened to what I had to say. After that my ninth grade students learned about ancient Rome and current events of the late 1970s. My classes at Hampstead Hill Junior High School consisted of blacks, whites, Koreans, and part of a native American tribe originally from Lumberton, North Carolina. In 1977 Hampstead Hill was probably the most racially diverse junior high school in Baltimore City. But I enforced the rules for all students, and the ninth graders respected me for it. While my teaching skills improved, I applied for a history teaching position at Virginia Beach, Virginia.

The Virginia Beach Director of Education seemed to be impressed with my skills and wished to hire me for the position of history teacher. My *dream job* was within reach. But by the first week of May I received a telephone call from Virginia Beach. The director informed me that a sixty-eight year old history teacher decided to continue teaching and the position was no longer available. I had to wait at least another year for that position to become available. As I was twenty-five years old and living with my parents, I could not wait any longer for a teaching position. I applied that summer repeatedly for a teaching position in Baltimore City public schools without any luck. When Elvis Presley died in August 1977, I took the Army Battery test and decided to enlist in the United States Army. At least the army wanted my services.

After passing all of the army tests in August, I became part of a surprising celebration in September. Brother Robert, who became nineteen years of age, married his high school sweetheart. I knew that the two of them were engaged but the hastiness of the event surprised me. But they tied the knot and their union produced two healthy sons later in life. In 1977 my parents had one child finally leave the nest. I followed my brother's example shortly after his wedding and that left the two youngest children at home.

Having aced the clerical part of the Army Battery test, I decided to pursue a military occupational specialty or MOS of personnel records clerk. I swore an oath to the United States Constitution on October 7th as an inactive reserve of the United States Army. On November 17th I departed for basic training at Fort Jackson, South Carolina as a private first class. I began my army career as an E-3 instead of an E-1 because of my college degree. After five weeks of basic training, I returned home for the holidays for two weeks and then reported back to base on January 4th 1978. I finished basic training in January, having survived the fifteen mile road march while carrying all of my possessions, and earned an expert marksman badge. Soon I became a squad leader in this platoon. As basic training ended at Fort Jackson, I trudged off to the other side of post and reported there for personnel records training. I had to type a minimum of twenty words per minute and to provide all of the upkeep of a military personnel record jacket or MPRJ for short. After seven weeks of training, I satisfied all of the US Army requirements to be a personnel records specialist. I then flew to Germany on the day after Easter in late March. Before I left Fort Jackson, I met a lovely young lady from Phillipsburg, New Jersey, who was in the US Army Reserves. We communicated through letter writing on a monthly basis and I hoped to see her while on leave in December. In Germany I saw sights and sounds that I had never previously experienced in life.

Arriving in Germany during the first full week of spring is

a treat. The trains which are extremely prompt there, take you to any place in the country that you wish to visit for a small fare. On my initial trip from Frankfurt to Heidelberg, I saw statuesque castles in the middle of the Rhine River, verdant valleys of terraced grape arbors, and magnificent tall green mountains. The train snaked around all of these features and stayed within view of not only the Rhine River, but also the Neckar River, which was my final destination. For security's sake long after I was discharged from the military, I will not reveal any specifics about the personnel company for whom I worked or the units that we serviced there. I will never betray the interests of my country intentionally or discuss the exact troop locations in Germany. But there were some details of my life at that time that can be shared.

I lived for two and one half years in a small town near the Neckar River. Occasionally I watched barges from different countries navigate the river and marveled at how the canal locks lifted or lowered barges to the proper elevation. When I arrived at my unit, there wasn't any time for such trivial things. The personnel company which requested my service, was preparing for a major inspection in April, and needed everyone's assistance to pass. We worked sixteen hours on weekdays and eight hours on Saturdays to prepare. I had been through four months of training and felt like I was being slammed to the mat. In April 1978, I received more bad news. I got a letter from dad, describing the mess left in Baltimore. I sold my car before I shipped out to Germany. Unfortunately I didn't transfer the title of the car to the new buyer. As the new owner had an accident, I was still liable. Fortunately dad intervened and the issue was settled in my favor. But refreshing change came in May, as the personnel company passed inspection.

May was a great time of the year to discover the sights of Germany. With weekends off and an extra day off for Memorial Day, I saw the sights. I encountered my first sergeant in a guesthouse near the barracks. A guesthouse is a German tavern and my first sergeant was slightly tipsy from drinking the local brand of beer. As I was reasonably sober and had a valid Maryland driving license, my first sergeant asked me to drive him home via the Autobahn, or German super highway. While driving eighty-five miles per hour, I saw headlights gaining quickly on the first sergeant's van. I instinctively decreased the vehicle's speed, as I thought it was the police. When my first sergeant informed me that there was no speed limit on the Autobahn, I got a quick glimpse of a Mercedes Benz being driven at one hundred miles per hour. The following week after this Autobahn adventure, I got promoted to specialist four, the same pay grade as corporal. With a college degree prior to enlistment, I was supposed to be promoted after four months of service. But the personnel company had more pressing needs, and when those needs were satisfied, immediately took care of other business. Now I was on cruise control and enjoyed German cuisine that summer.

Germany had potent beer, about thirteen percent alcohol by volume, and the wine was even more potent. Different regions of the country had festivals displaying their various products and the consumers voiced their opinions as to which beer or wine tasted best to them. There were also many exotic foods such as schnitzel, wurst, spatzle and sauerbraten. As the weather warmed the populace frequented more festivals in different locales in Germany. I thoroughly enjoyed the food and drink during that summer, but in August my singular mission for entering the US Army began to take shape. I wanted to earn a master's degree in human services while serving in the United States Army.

During that month I applied for acceptance into the master's degree program in human services at Boston University Overseas. In order to register for the course I was required to pass the Graduate Record Examination. I passed all three parts of the examination, even scoring at the 92nd percentile on the mathematics part. Taking a human services course in September, I earned an A- grade in Psychodiagnosis and paid just fifteen dollars to take the four credit graduate course. This was the main reason that I enlisted in the US Army at twenty-five years of age. I could serve my country and further my education while doing so.

After the course ended, I took an extended leave of absence in mid-December. I spent the weekend with my family, rented a car on Monday and traveled to Phillipsburg, New Jersey. I saw my twenty year old shapely, brunette friend and remained lovers daily until mid-January, when I took a return flight to Germany. By that time we were engaged with a September wedding date. After reaching the personnel company, news traveled quickly back to me.

In February 1979 my parents traveled to Flemington, New Jersey to meet my fiance's mother and stepfather. The meeting among the four of them went exceptionally well, and my parents saw the white Methodist church on the Delaware River, which was the wedding destination. By the end of February all of those plans were dissolved. My fiance had a miscarriage with my baby and sent me a *Dear John* letter through the mail. The letter with an eight cent stamp on the envelope also included an engagement ring. My former fiance said "Your baby is dead and we are through. Here's your ring back." I was stunned and extremely hurt. I was determined to discover what really went wrong, the next time that I ventured to New Jersey. In the meantime, there was work to do for the US Army.

In 1979 my job consisted of maintaining over two hundred officer personnel records, and typing or penciling any changes to those records. In addition to my main job function, I arose early and performed physical training daily. Physical training included many calisthenics and numerous miles run in formation. After completion of these physical tasks, one showered and dressed in the appropriate uniform for work. Then one cleaned his or her own billets area, as well as common areas such as latrines, hallways, or entertainment rooms. Then one walked across the street to the chow hall for breakfast and returned to one's job in personnel records.

By May I took my second four credit graduate course entitled Counseling: Philosophy and Theory and did not finish the course until August. Again I earned an A- grade in a human services course. That summer our personnel company experienced a major change. We changed company commanders and received a new commander who was *gung ho*. Anyone who has watched the show M.A.S.H. on television knows the meaning of that term. After one month as company commander, he summoned me to his office. With many soldiers in our company receiving military discipline, I had no idea what to expect from him.

The new company commander wanted me to apply for *Officer Candidate School* as he felt that I had all of the necessary qualifications to be a commissioned officer in the United States Army. A commissioned officer in the US Army ranged in rank from second lieutenant up to general and always had to be saluted by enlisted personnel in outdoor areas. A commissioned officer outranked all enlisted personnel even a command sergeant major or E-9. Commissioned officers also outranked warrant officers and were to be saluted by them in public places as well. If this opportunity had existed prior to this time I would have applied for the program. But seeing the peace time army dwindle in numbers, especially career promotions from captain to major, it looked like all of my efforts would be in vain. Just like certain businesses and schools in the late 1970s, the US Army was downsizing as well. As I worked in officer records and saw the officer promotion list from the Department of the Army on a periodic basis, I saw careers end for certain commissioned officers. Even some United States Military Academy graduates were encouraged to resign their commission and accept an honorable discharge for time of service, after being denied a career promotion to major for the first time. Knowing that my credentials in the United States Army were not up to West Point standards, I withdrew my name from consideration for *Officer Candidate School*.

In September I returned to Baltimore, using all of the available leave time that I had accrued by then. Having recently found out that the overseas service tour of Germany was reduced to two years duration, I had just over six months left to serve in the US Army overseas. But while on leave, there was a mystery to solve in New Jersey.

I rented a car in Baltimore and arrived at my former fiance's house unexpectedly. She was taking a bath when I arrived and we soon made love. She then drove me to her parents' house in Flemington. Her actions were totally inconsistent, as she had not seen her mother or stepfather in many months. After

I renewed my acquaintance with them, her parents drove me back to the vehicle as night descended upon Phillipsburg. I snuck past the vehicle toward the house and noticed two naked figures illuminated in the kitchen. With the pickup truck parked in the driveway, I finally realized the truth about my ex-fiance. Before I could take another step, my ex-fiance aimed a shotgun at me from the kitchen window and said "If you take one more step Chris Harrison, I will blow your head off." I quietly slipped into the rental car and left the state of New Jersey as quickly as possible. Her mother later wrote to me and informed me that her daughter had married this other man after my stormy visit. The following year my ex-fiancé got a divorce and begged me for a second chance. I told her very painfully "Anyone who pulls a shotgun on me, gets no second chance. Our chance to be together is over and you made that choice." I returned to Germany with a renewed sense of purpose after the mystery was solved.

The month of November in 1979 was actually a good one for me. Our personnel company trained in the field for a week while servicing line units. In the field I got promoted to specialist five, the same pay grade as sergeant. I was now considered a non-commissioned officer or NCO in the US Army without formal training. An NCO is an enlisted person who has attained the rank of E-5 and above and is generally in a supervisory position. The only exception to this rule is a corporal, whose *hard stripe* assured one of an E-5 leadership position. While our personnel company was in the field, a Baltimore native and Forest Park graduate shook hands with Major General George Patton Junior, son of the famous World War II general. The general was supposed to inspect our entire company but only made it to the perimeter gate. The gate guard was so impressive that General Patton told the officer-in-charge, that he had seen enough and left the area. This particular Forest Park graduate did not wash his hands for the next week saying, "General Patton shook my hand." I guess it was a good month for Baltimore native sons stationed in Germany. Now it was time for the personnel company to return to the barracks.

That particular holiday season was the first time that I was away from my immediate family. But I counted the days left to serve in Germany with just over three months left of my overseas service tour. While these events took place in my life, Iran and its Islamic fundamentalists took American hostages and the US Army was on high alert. Most of the soldiers that I spoke to about this situation were ready, willing, and able to go to war against Iran. Meanwhile I met a busty German barmaid, who was twenty years old. We had a long and tempestuous romance for the next six months. With a fraulein taking care of my daily needs, I extended my tour of service in Germany until September 1980. At that time I had only fourteen months left to serve in the US Army.

An earth shattering issue in January 1980 started the new decade. The Soviet Union invaded Afghanistan and all of our troops were put on high alert. President Jimmy Carter, who was commander-in-chief of all armed forces, warned the Soviet Union, "To get out of Afghanistan or else…" For many days our troops were anxious, but eventually the high level of the alert subsided. In February a winter sports highlight also shook the foundation of the world. The United States Olympic men's ice hockey team with a roster of college players, defeated the powerful Soviet Union by one goal in the Olympic semi-final medals round. The Soviet Union had not lost in men's hockey in twenty years. They were the most dominant team in the history of the Winter Olympics. The game itself started at 9 P.M. eastern standard time that Friday night or 3 A.M. Saturday morning in Germany. The *Armed Forces Network* carried the hockey game in its entirety. Every time that I fell asleep and reawakened the hockey score was different. That particular Saturday the host Germans treated American soldiers as if we were celebrities. The Germans were in awe of American tenacity in the 1980 Winter Olympics against overwhelming odds. I can honestly say on that particular day, every American stationed in Germany was just proud to be one.

Meanwhile I continued my whirlwind romance with my busty barmaid girlfriend. But I ended it briefly, as she cheated on me. I was hurt badly but she begged me for a second chance. At this time I made a proposal to her. I asked her if she remained faithful to me for two months, that we would become engaged. For her part she remained faithful for the next two months, and due to her loyalty, she had an engagement party with a gold ring. Her German friends and my barracks roommates attended as well. By midnight everyone was drunk or asleep except my fiance. She drank everyone *under the table*, and in Germany that was a daunting task. With beer high in percentage of alcohol volume, it was a miracle for anyone to remain sober. But my fiancé drank as long as she desired to do so.

The engagement was short-lived. Two weeks later my fiance disappeared for a day and then telephoned me at the barracks, to inform me that she had an abortion. She also informed me that she was two months pregnant and that the baby was mine. As infuriated as I was about this issue the following week my temper exploded. After I finished physical training one morning, I walked to my fiance's apartment and found her in bed with another man. She was physically everything that I ever wanted in a woman, but did not know how to love one person. Needless to say our relationship ended at that point. During the rest of the summer I tried to make amends with my roommates. All three had been patient with me during those tumultuous love affairs.

As a group my three roommates were the best three friends that I've ever had in my life. My first roommate was a married Korean-American from Hackensack, New Jersey who just produced a beautiful baby girl. He earned an associate's degree in business administration, worked in the computer room, and performed personnel transactions on all service members. My second roommate from Denver, Colorado was an unmarried Mexican-American, who loved the Denver Broncos. He also had an associate's degree in business administration, and was the supply sergeant's assistant. My third roommate was a crazy Caucasian from West Orange, New Jersey who loved Leonard Skynnard and Jethro Tull. He was a dedicated personnel records specialist with an extremely high accuracy rate in daily transactions. All three were neat and clean roommates, who made living in a foreign country bearable for me for two and one half years. I certainly would not have survived Germany without their help.

With summer rapidly disappearing in Germany, I took several farewell photographs of Heidelberg including the cobblestone streets, the streetcars, and the main castle guarding the town's original entrance. With the stunningly high mountains and the blue waves of the Neckar River in the background, the photographs were extremely scenic. But

September arrived and twenty-two of us in this particular personnel company returned to the United States during that month. Some soldiers were discharged from the United States Army and others were sent to a new duty station. On September 22nd I left Germany early in the morning in fifty degree weather and arrived at New Jersey at noon in eighty degree weather. My dad picked me up and drove me home. I used thirty days of leave and reported to Fort Campbell, Kentucky in October.

During my leave of absence, I got an opportunity to renew acquaintances with my immediate family. Brother Robert had bought a house in Dundalk on his automobile mechanic's earnings. His wife Laura expected a baby in December. Sister Janet graduated from Dundalk Community College *summa cum laude* and earned an associate's degree in computer science. Janet then began employment as a computer specialist. Meanwhile brother Michael had begun his senior year of high school. Meanwhile I had some business to complete while at home.

Though I failed to progress at the educational level during my last year in Germany, I added to my savings account every month. With over two thousand dollars in savings, dad and I went car shopping. Eventually I settled on a 1980 Chevrolet Monza sedan. Dad told me "With all of the driving that you will do in the next year, you're going to need something that is reliable." He was right of course, but with thirty-six months of payments, I had a lot of work to do. But I took my new silver car to the beach, dated a lot of women, and prepared for the last thirteen months of military service.

During the third week of October, I departed for Fort Campbell, Kentucky, located on the Kentucky and Tennessee state lines. Driving south through Virginia to that ultimate destination, I saw beautiful mountains with all of their fall foliage. While driving south on Interstate 81, there were colorful hues of orange, red, brown and gold on the deciduous trees, and an occasional evergreen as well. The journey was truly a magnificent spectacle. When I bought gasoline or food, the people were friendly in my travels. I was a single man with a new car, and liked traveling south. I was ready for change at the age of twenty-eight.

The following day I arrived at Fort Campbell and met my new commander. He was a Texan, with a deep drawl, and gave me an overview of what to expect at my new duty assignment. I was assigned at that time to the 101st Adjutant General Company. Being a non-commissioned officer, I shared a large room and adjoining shower with another NCO. At the office, I supervised a small personnel section in one of the four records teams there. In contrast to officer records, this section contained military records of soldiers who were undergoing court martials, bars to reenlistment, or other forms of military justice. I met all of my co-workers one day and worked with them the next.

Fort Campbell, Kentucky is the proud home of the 101st Air Assault Division. While running many miles in formation on post, one could literally run from Tennessee to Kentucky on a daily basis. Most of the post was in Tennessee, but the post office was located in Kentucky, and thus became the state of residence. After one month of working and running, my new company assembled a formation in my behalf. I received the Army Commendation Medal for service in the Federal Republic of Germany, received the Overseas Service Ribbon for completion of an overseas service tour, and received the

Good Conduct Medal for three years of performing my duty for the United States Army. Suddenly I had a few medals pinned on my chest to accompany an expert marksmanship badge.

As December brought cold weather, I planned to spend some of the holidays in Baltimore. By working Christmas, I got an extra day off for New Year's Day 1981. With four consecutive days off, two friends and I drove through a huge snowstorm on New Year's day and arrived at Baltimore. I took the other two soldiers home and picked them up that Sunday to return to Fort Campbell. Fortunately the weather improved and it was clear skies for our return trip to post.

The year 1981 was to be my year, as I only had three hundred twenty days of military service left to fulfill my enlistment contract. During that year I met new friends and ventured to Nashville at least twice a month. Nashville, which was only fifty-five miles from post, had tons of country music talent. My friends and I watched the entertainers perform at the *honky tonk bars*. My friends and I also sampled the wares of the Tennessee State Fair and rode the mechanical bull at *Mickey Gilley's Bar*, as seen on the movie *Urban Cowboy*. In addition to everything else in Nashville, there was Vanderbilt University and the Parthenon Art Building in beautiful Centennial Park. The biggest new attraction in 1981 was the wave pool. Many of the soldiers went there and thoroughly enjoyed this new type of pool. During that summer I visited my parents at the Outer Banks of North Carolina for three days. With all of this driving, I traveled over thirty thousand miles in one year with the new vehicle. But I saw many sights.

Back at Fort Campbell I continued my regular routine, and took a graduate course every fourteen weeks during that year. The graduate courses that I took were from Murray State University's graduate division at Fort Campbell. During the year I earned nine credits in three courses with a B average. With financial constraints a major issue, I never completed course work for a master's degree in human services.

In the spring of 1981 Fort Campbell received a new post adjutant commander. He was Pete Dawkins, the 1958 *Heisman Trophy* winner from the United States Military Academy. At forty-three years of age, General Dawkins became one of the youngest brigadier generals in the history of the United States Army. Being youthful and athletic, he galloped past many formations and waved at the pace setters like me. A pace setter sets the running pace for the company's formation. Since I was neither the fastest nor the slowest runner in the company, I usually set a good pace. Meanwhile the noncommissioned officers catered a luncheon in General Dawkins' behalf. I actually met the general and shook hands with him. Unlike my old Forest Park friend in Germany, I washed my hands after meeting Brigadier General Dawkins.

The summer of 1981 had so many activities, that I did not have time for relationships. As November neared and my service commitment expired, a personnel clerk issued a warning to me saying "You won't last six months out there." I told her that I would never reenlist for the US Army. She replied "It is not the army that you'll have to worry about. You will be married in the next six months." Even though I liked this particular clerk, I thought her warning was ludicrous. In the past I had failed at every relationship with the opposite sex.

On Friday the 13th of November, I took three days of terminal leave and exited from the US Army. Three of my new friends at Fort Campbell brought another vehicle to Baltimore and celebrated my return to civilian life that weekend. Then these three friends from Cincinnati, Daytona Beach, and Wilmington, Delaware returned to Fort Campbell on Monday. I was at home with my parents for the first time since the 1950s. Robert and his wife Laura prepared to celebrate their son's first birthday. Sister Janet married her fiancé in October and I flew in for the occasion. By the time my enlistment in the US Army ended, Janet and her husband lived in an apartment. Youngest brother Michael joined the United States Marine Corps that summer and finished his advanced training. Then mom, dad, Michael and I had dinner at the Brentwood Inn, and Michael left for overseas duty. It was just the three of us at home like the old days.

With an honorable discharge from active duty in one hand and a bachelor's degree in the other, I looked for a job after the Thanksgiving holiday with no luck. Inflation was at a high level in addition to the unemployment rate. As bad as the year 1975 was for finding work, November of 1981 was even worse. But I secured a job as a clerk-typist for a supply company with machine parts. I was the only applicant that knew how to type on a manual typewriter and got the job. At four dollars an hour it wasn't much, but I had to start somewhere in society.

Meanwhile an old army friend from Boston, telephoned me at home. He was stationed at Fort Meade, Maryland, so we planned a New Year's Eve celebration at a known Baltimore bar and grill. I brought one of my sister's girl friends from the neighborhood to meet my army buddy to see if they might click. However, as the clock approached midnight and the start of 1982, I was in store for a pleasant surprise. The female cook behind the bar kissed me longer and harder than anyone I had ever met in my life. Soon my life changed forever.

CHAPTER VII

GETTING MARRIED AND "GOING POSTAL"

That kiss on New Year's Day became the first of many between me and my new lady Faye. Faye was an attractive brunette at fifty years of age who had four grown children and many young grandchildren. She was overweight and only five foot three inches tall, but had a magnificent heart. We had met when I taught at Hampstead Hill Junior High School in 1977 and she was impressed by my appearance. She always said that "I was her knight in shining armor." Now I knew that she liked me for my personality. The supply boss for whom I worked, invited me and a date to the Hibernian Club Roast in January. Faye and I attended the event. We continued dating and had a late date on the occasion of my thirtieth birthday. This necessitated a mad rush by me to my parents' house at 3 A.M. That was because dad worked until 3 A.M. at the downtown post office, and I wished to keep peace while I lived on Loganview Drive. But Faye thought that it was sad for a thirty year old man to rush home in the middle of the night. Soon that situation changed drastically for the foreseeable future.

After trying to explain my future intentions to mom, I

decided to *throw caution to the wind* and moved in with Faye. We moved into the second floor of a row house on Lombard Street and lived for the next two years at that address. I also thought about what the clerk at Fort Campbell said, and realized that four months after ending my enlistment with the US Army, I lived with a fifty year old woman. Faye and I were poor but our love was boundless. At this time, I quit my job at the supply company after failing to get a raise and started a similar job at a Pikesville cemetery making more money. Unfortunately that job ended and I got laid off in November. Before that occurred, I saw an advertisement in the Baltimore Sunpapers for wrestling coach. After applying for that position, I became the varsity and junior varsity wrestling coach at Loyola High School. I felt that God was on my side and this was an opportunity to display my skills as a wrestling coach.

Loyola High School in 1982 had an athletic director who doubled as the varsity basketball coach. So basketball was the main event in the winter sports season at Loyola, and wrestling was not a priority at that school. Even the football team enjoyed greater access to the weight training room than the wrestling team during the winter season. Nevertheless, I had two senior co-captains who were glad to meet me and have a wrestling team that year. These two co-captains were as gritty a duo of wrestlers as I have ever seen. With their leadership and my coaching, Loyola struggled for fifth place out of eight schools in the Baltimore Catholic Tournament at Archbishop Curley High School. As I was a Curley alumnus, this was a homecoming event for me in December, 1982. Loyola's wrestling team struggled throughout the season and had a losing record.

While I struggled as Loyola's wrestling coach, home life

was great. Faye was a great cook and we ate well at home despite our lack of income. She loved me more than anything in the world and I finally popped the question after *living in sin* for a year. Although Faye loved me she was reluctant to accept my offer. As her first husband of twenty-nine years was so abusive, she was cautious. Nevertheless we made plans for an April wedding, although not in a Catholic church. But in late February I prepared Loyola's grapplers for the Maryland Scholastic Association Wrestling Tournament.

Loyola High School has had some great sports teams throughout its long history, but this particular wrestling team was not one of them. However this group of wrestlers was a very resilient bunch. Our one co-captain and 167 pound wrestler finished fourth in his weight class out of twenty-eight wrestlers. The other co-captain, a 145 pound wrestler, finished sixth in his weight class. He received a sixth place trophy and a place on the podium. Our *super sophomore* at 108 pounds, finished fourth place in his weight class at the MSA tournament as well. Loyola High School earned fifty-three team points and a tie for eleventh place out of twenty-eight schools in the MSA Wrestling Tournament in 1983. Loyola would have finished in the top ten wrestling schools of this tournament with two more individual wins. I was very proud of this resilient group of wrestlers. I did a credible job too, as I was invited to return as wrestling coach with a raise in salary. As wrestling season ended, I experienced dramatic change.

My fiancé invited me to meet a Lutheran pastor for a possible church wedding. The pastor reluctantly agreed to perform the ceremony despite our age difference. His conditions were that I learn all of the basic tenets of the Lutheran Church in six weeks. After completing bible study, I had the daunting task of introducing Faye to my mother. As I had not spoken to mother in nearly a year, I was prepared for anything. But grandmother Lapka was at my mother's house and greeted Faye as she arrived there. Grandmother Lapka, my mother's mother, said "Welcome to the family Faye. I'm sure that you will make my grandson happy." She then hugged Faye and they embraced each other. My mother then fell in line and verbally accepted Faye as well. We ate dinner together and prepared for an April 23rd wedding.

The day of our wedding was a cloudy, rainy one. But we were happy and had a simple Lutheran ceremony and a simple reception on Foster Avenue, where Faye's oldest son Andy lived. Only immediate family attended the reception and Andy had enough cold cuts and drinks for everyone there. Naturally we got to know one another quickly and the families bonded well. Faye and I left and then drove to *Busch Gardens* in Williamsburg, Virginia for our honeymoon. During the entire time it rained constantly, but we thoroughly enjoyed the plays, rides, and food there. We then returned to Baltimore and sunshine. We were poor but happy. But in May 1983, the fickle finger of fate blessed me with a great opportunity.

The United States Postal Service finally agreed to hire me as a part-time flexible carrier after passing the clerk-carrier examination the previous year. At a starting salary of over ten dollars an hour, I was pleased to begin my new career. I delivered mail until the third week of June while working at the Dundalk post office. While driving a postal vehicle one day, I spilled a drink near the collection mail obtained earlier that day. In an attempt to prevent the mail from being soaked, I turned my attention to the back seat, and the vehicle jumped a curb. Then the vehicle struck a McDonald's sign due to my negligence. As there was no damage to the vehicle, I was relieved at this time. Then I apologized to the McDonald's manager and he said that the extra sign was of no consequence. But it mattered greatly to the US Postal Service, and they terminated my employment on July 6th, citing me for an *at-fault accident* during the probationary period of employment.

I then filed an equal employment opportunity complaint against the US Postal Service in Baltimore and specifically against the postmaster there. The US Postal Service later agreed to reinstate me as a mail handler in a non-driving capacity in August rather than a hearing and possibly a court date. I agreed to the conditions and dropped my EEO complaint. At this point in time I worked the midnight shift and made a good salary while doing it.

As a mail handler at the main post office in Baltimore, I loaded and unloaded trucks nightly. As a part-time flexible mail handler I earned a good salary, worked ten hours a night and six nights a week. I earned a lot of money quickly and immediately paid for the 1980 Chevrolet Monza. I then completed my ninety day probationary period satisfactorily and got the job done. Now I had union representation for every task. Meanwhile I coached wrestling at Loyola High.

As the year 1984 began, everything headed in a positive direction. However all of that positive feeling changed, when I reported to work on a Saturday night. In fact I nearly died. As I made a left turn into the employees' parking garage, I narrowly avoided being struck by a vehicle speeding in the opposite direction. Though the posted speed limit was five miles per hour and I traveled at a speed of at least ten miles per hour, the same speeding vehicle followed my vehicle and *tailgated* me throughout the garage. As I attempted to back my car into a parking space, the same vehicle nearly struck my vehicle again.

This time I exited my car and looked at the driver, who was black and said "What the hell is your problem?" He replied "You better worry about your job white boy." I then answered "I'm worried about my car right now." Then I opened the door to my vehicle and returned to the driver's seat. The other driver then knocked on my door. As I shoved the door quickly to repel him from my car, he retreated quickly, and then brutally stabbed my left leg with a hidden bayonet. With the main artery in my left leg lacerated and blood spewed everywhere, he punched me in the jaw. I'm sure that his plan was for me to remain unconscious and bleed to death. But I pretended to be unconscious which was a wise decision at the time. As he exited my car with a blood smeared bayonet, I opened my eyes wide enough to observe his vehicle and the license plate. I felt as if my next breath might be my last.

After the assailant departed from the parking garage, I drove my car to a *no parking zone* near the security guard shack. A maintenance employee saw the end of the stabbing incident and came to my rescue. He helped me out of the car and into the guard shack. This hero who happened to be black, saved my life that night. The security guards called for an ambulance to transport me to Johns Hopkins Hospital. There they operated on my left leg and didn't allow me to return home until late that Sunday morning. For the next week I had internal bleeding and experienced much pain. I did not work at the post office and I could not coach wrestling at Loyola High School. The assailant reported to work that Monday morning at the main post office with his lawyer beside him. Needless to say, he was read his rights and temporarily incarcerated. At his trial he and I exchanged words again.

By the end of January, I reported to work in a *light duty status* at the main post office, using a crutch to support my left leg. I kept my wounded leg elevated on a chair and typed or filed whatever paper work was necessary at the doctor's office there. I then ventured to Loyola High School and greeted the team upon my return as wrestling coach. My last hurrah as coach was at a wrestling match between Loyola and Curley at my old alma mater. When Loyola's 185 pound wrestler pinned Curley's wrestler, he gave me a hug while I was still on a crutch. The crowd at Curley's gymnasium gave us both a standing ovation. Nevertheless Curley easily won the match and Loyola's season continued in a downward spiral. By the end of February though, I was working full-time at the post office and coaching wrestling without the use of crutches. At the 1984 MSA Wrestling Tournament, Loyola High School finished in a dismal twenty-first place of twenty-eight schools in the tournament. I was then informed by the Loyola High School athletic director that my services were no longer needed for the following year.

However my marriage was strong at the time and the left leg improved quickly. I continued to grow stronger physically and attended my assailant's trial in May. My assailant was convicted of assault and battery with a deadly weapon. He lost his job and received an eighteen month prison sentence. But I suffered emotionally as a result of this incident. For many years I carried a baseball bat with nails through it for protection while driving my automobile. In my world, it was *kill or be killed* for a long period of time. But my wife understood how I felt and that is all that really mattered to me.

By late summer 1984, Faye and I moved to Baltimore County near the Middle River area and rented a two bedroom townhouse. We were glad to leave the city and relocate near the woods. Now that I was a full-time regular mail handler, I paid a little more rent and drove a new car. However, I failed the postal inspector examination that year. Upon completion of this examination, I realized some of the mistakes that I had made and that it was probably the most difficult examination that I had ever attempted to pass. Furthermore, I had to wait another year before I could retake this examination. To become a postal inspector was the main reason that I applied for postal employment. Having strong mathematics skills and a proficiency in firearms, I wanted to become a postal inspector and earn a great salary while doing so. Since I was prepared to travel for the United States Postal Inspection Service, I felt a long vacation was needed at this time.

In spring 1985 Faye and I took a week long trip through southwest Virginia and Tennessee. We both loved the mountains and deeply desired to move there. We also liked the country and the people that lived there. We visited Roanoke, Virginia and I applied for a mail handler position that might become available at that facility. After that we returned to Baltimore and the main post office.

In fall 1985 I finally achieved a milestone. I passed the postal inspector examination with a 77% ranking. Dad still worked at the main post office and was amazed at this development. I was ready to travel wherever needed. At the same time, a black female clerk who had befriended me, received a passing score of 72% on the same examination. I wanted both of us to get promoted to postal inspector but fate was not on my side.

On November 5, 1985, the Roanoke River overflowed its

banks and flooded the entire Roanoke Valley. By the second week of November, the Roanoke post office requested my records as a new employee with a reporting date of December 7th. The Baltimore postal supervisor broke the news saying, "Your record file is heading to Roanoke, Virginia and maybe it is under five feet of water there." So Faye and I packed up all of our furniture and her son Andy drove the moving van to Roanoke. Andy stayed with us initially and later settled in Roanoke. We made arrangements with Cinnamon Ridge Townhouses in Roanoke County and started a new life. With local residents losing their homes due to the flooding, it was not an easy task to rent a townhouse in Roanoke. But we applied for one by mid-November and began a new lease by December 1st. I was ready for a change and got it. I always loved the state of Virginia, but never had a job to live in it. Now I secured a job in Virginia and waited for a better one as postal inspector.

As I began work in December, I started at the bottom of the seniority list or one day junior to the mail handler with the least seniority at the Roanoke Main Post Office. Since the previous employee had a seniority date of March 31, 1985, my seniority date became April 1, 1985, as I transferred within my craft in the US Postal Service. However, I became a part-time flexible mail handler again with one major difference from the Baltimore post office. In Baltimore I served a ninety day probationary period as a new employee. As I worked previously at another postal facility in the same craft, another probationary period was unnecessary. So I worked the midnight shift again, and tried to show my new employers that I was a worthwhile employee. I did this for two reasons. The first reason was that I always want to make a positive impression when starting a new job. The second reason was that I was still a postal inspector candidate and needed assistance to obtain that position. As a part-time flexible mail handler, I worked six nights a week and sometimes twelve hours a night, in an attempt to process all of the incoming mail during the month of December. It was an ordeal for me, but more so for my wife.

This was Faye's first Christmas away from her three daughters and she did not know anyone in Roanoke. With the wintry weather upon us and dark days, she had a miserable month. But Faye always cooked great meals for Andy and me and kept the townhouse immaculate. Before Christmas, Andy started a job for Roanoke Fruit and Produce, and more money swelled the family's budget. On a very dismal Christmas I worked twelve hours and observed late packages being processed on conveyor belts. But on the last week of December, I was compensated with the biggest check that I had ever earned. Faye and I finally got into the holiday spirit. As New Year's day approached, Andy found a new girlfriend who was older than him. Andy spent a lot of time with his woman when he wasn't working, but Faye found a new friend in Andy's beau as well. Soon Andy lived with his girlfriend, but Faye found a new social outlet with the members of her family. In many ways however, it was the two of us in a new location.

Roanoke was a city of about a hundred thousand residents, but with larger numbers of people in the surrounding areas of Roanoke County, Salem, and Vinton. At the south end of the city amid the Blue Ridge Mountains on Mill Mountain is a large, shining star atop of that mountain. Hence Roanoke is referred to as the *Star City of the South*. Of course, the star with its presence, has guided airline traffic to and from the city. The valley itself has two very prominent malls, a zoo atop of Mill Mountain, a spacious civic center, the one and only *Hotel Roanoke*, and other excellent restaurants. Known for southern cuisine, these restaurants have breakfasts loaded with country ham, grits and biscuits with country gravy. Dinners include great steaks, barbequed ribs, and fried chicken. With *Red Lobster* and *Olive Garden* located here too, there is a wide variety of cuisine. The people in the Roanoke Valley are generally friendly with a few exceptions.

The exceptions to the friendly people of the south were some of the crew that worked at the main post office in Roanoke. My supervisors generally liked me, but some of my co-workers repelled my friendly advances. These people were part of a clique of local high school graduates who resented anyone from the outside invading their territory. As I was from north of Roanoke and a *damn Yankee* who looked Hispanic, I was not welcomed by the clique. Fortunately the rest of the south was not populated by the clique, and generally Faye and I developed new friendships. I learned to ignore the clique and only spoke to one of them when they spoke to me. Being a very independent person by nature and having accomplished a few things in life, I didn't need any type of adolescent peer pressure behavior in my daily routine.

By May 1986 I became a full-time regular mail handler again, with an initial job description of third-class mail conveyor belt mail handler on the midnight shift. Now that I had a regular position again, I eventually applied for a home loan under the provisions of the G.I. Bill. As summer began my home life improved as well. Faye and I used the Olympic sized pool at Cinnamon Ridge Townhouses and met many people there. I soon decided to get a better vehicle as well. I opted for the 1986 Pontiac Grand Am, which I later discovered was *Motor Trend Magazine's Car of the Year*. In the absence of my father, I finally made a wise decision in an automobile purchase. At this time in my life I hesitated to buy a home, because of the possibility of relocation as a postal inspector. But after discussing the matter with a realtor, Faye and I settled on a three bedroom, one bath house in northeast Roanoke City. This was the first time that Faye and I ever owned a home and we were delighted with the prospect. This occasion became one of the happiest moments of our lives in September 1986. But life goes on and so did the two of us.

Christmas of 1986 was much more pleasant than the previous one. We had a great neighbor, with a wife and nine year old son, in our Monterey Hills subdivision and they ate Christmas dinner at our home. I had made a few friends at work and they attended as well. Andy brought his girlfriend with her family and everyone had a truly great time. Faye was such a great cook and everyone truly enjoyed the food. Life was good and most of my days were happy ones. But a new year brings new issues.

By spring 1987, after my initial application was delayed due to physical issues such as a hernia or bayonet scar, the postal inspector recruiter finally visited Roanoke to interview me for that position. The recruiter who was a Caucasian female and an EAS 25 in the US Postal Inspection Service from Bala Cynwyd, Pennsylvania, claimed that it was her initial visit to Roanoke. She visited my home and conducted her interview in my wife's presence. After observing my olive skin and black hair, the postal inspector asked "Do you speak Spanish?" As I passed three courses in high school and a course in college, I replied "Yes I do." She then asked another question which totally shocked me, saying "Of course you are Hispanic, aren't you?" I replied steadfastly "No, I am not." The postal inspector with a crestfallen face replied "Well, there are other opportunities in the United States Postal Service." I glared at her and stammered, "This is the only position that I've ever wished to attain in the postal service. What are you trying to tell me?" The postal inspector then broke off the interview and ignored my question.

This same postal inspector then observed the main post office in Roanoke in operation and complained about the lack of female supervision there. As a result of this postal inspector's visit and observations, a flood of Equal Employment Opportunity complaints by female employees occurred shortly thereafter in Roanoke. Due to my age the possibility of becoming a postal inspector at that time became remote. A postal inspector must retire at fifty-five years of age with a minimum of twenty years of service. When I became thirty-six years old in February 1988, I was no longer eligible for that position. So I was living on borrowed time in 1987.

In the interim, I contacted my black female friend from Baltimore, who had passed the same postal inspector examination. She had been to the pistol firing range in Quantico, Virginia and failed to fire a forty-five caliber pistol. This was due to the weakness in her grip while attempting to fire the pistol. The postal inspector recruiters then aggressively pursued her candidacy, giving her strength exercises to improve her grip. Despite her previous lack of knowledge of the weapon, she passed the pistol firing course. I was happy about my friend's good fortune but frustrated about my own candidacy. But September of 1987 quickly caused one to forget one's own problems.

Grandmother Lapka died in Baltimore and all of the family members attended the funeral, even from my part of Virginia. With the death of my grandmother and my father's recently retirement from the postal service, my parents sold the house in Dundalk and relocated to the Outer Banks of North Carolina. Mom had retired that summer from the Social Security Administration with an *early out* after twenty years of government service and was prepared to travel. The two of them settled in Salvo, a small town on Pea Island, which was a narrow strip of beaches south of Nags Head, North Carolina. My parents lived there for the next seven years and dad caught many fish. Logan Village had now lost two of its original residents.

Back in Roanoke, Virginia, we prepared for our third Christmas and I prepared for litigation against the postal inspection service. In February I became thirty-six years of age and was now ineligible for the position of postal inspector. The next day I filed an Equal Employment Opportunity complaint for *reverse discrimination*. I had scored a higher grade on the US Postal Inspector Examination than a certain black female recruit. Additionally I was a veteran who had attained previous firearms proficiency. With my mathematics skills and teaching experience, I felt that I was the better candidate and filed a lawsuit. The outcome of this case was not decided for years. In the interim, I completed payment of the social security deposits that the government withdrew from me during four years of military service. The result of this action was that my retirement date for federal service was changed from 2013 to 2009. I was happy about this development, but shocked about other news affecting the Harrison family.

Brother Robert and his wife Laura separated after eleven

years of marriage due to irreconcilable differences. The couple had produced two sons and there was considerable family uproar. Robert had visited Roanoke and liked the area especially Smith Mountain Lake. By 1989 Robert placed a deposit on a five acre tract of land on Blackwater River near Smith Mountain Lake. The Harrison family was steadily moving south.

In the years of 1988 and 1989, I made payments on the house and car while Faye and I enjoyed the scenery. As one peered out of the kitchen window, one saw a small hill in the rear of our yard and beyond that the magnificence of Read Mountain in all of its splendor. With money and food no longer major issues in our daily lives, we made the most of the situation at hand. I was happy with my personal life and with the inauguration of our new president George H.W. Bush. He was a war hero, college graduate, and college baseball player. He was the main reason that I switched political party allegiance to the Republican party.

With the inception of 1990 and the beginning of a new decade, I became greatly annoyed at the neighbor's son, who was now thirteen years of age. He returned home daily from school at 3 P.M. and bounced the basketball, disturbing my daytime sleep. As his basketball backboard was just thirty feet from my bedroom, even earplugs could not stifle the vibrations on the blacktopped basketball court. Then he started playing golf on our front yard and I built a chain link fence to prevent him from doing that. With a fence in our front and rear yard, we became prisoners in our own house and determined to buy another one. In May, Faye and I sold our city home and bought a country house.

In May 1990, Faye and I bought a house in the small

town of Blue Ridge in Botetourt County, which was just ten miles from downtown Roanoke. The house itself contained twelve hundred square feet of living space on one floor with two big bedrooms and two full bathrooms. We had a large screened-in-porch adjacent to the country kitchen, and a deck on the side of the house next to the study. The deck was just twenty feet from a small stream, which was one of our property dividers. The other two property dividers were an access road that led to our gravel driveway and Highway #460. We had a triangular tract of land on approximately one acre. We had no immediate neighbors to torment us so we were happy. Faye did say something very peculiar when we moved to the country. She said "This is the last house that I will live with you Harrison. This will be my final resting place." I could understand her reasoning to some extent, as we had lived in five different residences during our eight year relationship. Of course in 1990 I hoped that Faye would live for many years.

By that summer Andy had a new girlfriend in his life, a twenty year old beauty from southeast Roanoke. Andy was thirty-six years old by now, but realized that age was just a number as evidenced by his mother's marriage to me. In October 1990 Andy married his new love interest. Faye and I were happy for him and hoped that they would have a happy marriage. On the postal front I had a federal hearing against the postal inspectors during the month of November in the state of Pennsylvania.

Faye and I drove to Bala Cynwyd, Pennsylvania and presented my Equal Employment Opportunity complaint to a federal magistrate there. At the hearing I was represented by a prominent Roanoke lawyer whom I had chosen. I felt that our side had presented a substantial argument for *reverse discrimination* on the basis of race and sex. I did not hear any news for a while as to the decision of the federal magistrate concerning this hearing. When I did hear about the ruling, the federal magistrate ruled in favor of the US Postal Service. But I still had one more card to play and that was a trial in federal court. During the waiting phase of this ruling, I entertained my family on Thanksgiving Day.

On Thanksgiving, mom, dad, and grandmother Harrison visited Faye and me at our country home. Grandmother Harrison had dementia and lived in an assisted living facility in North Carolina. I was really pleased to see her but the talk of that particular day was the weather. The mercury reached seventy-two degrees and we all ate Thanksgiving dinner on the porch. I cannot recall a warmer Thanksgiving day. We all celebrated the holiday and basked in the abundant sunshine. It was truly a magnificent event for all. The following week the weather turned cold and remained that way during the rest of winter.

But it didn't remain cold overseas. In January 1991, the United States went to war against Iraq for annexing Kuwait, one of America's best allies in the petroleum industry. In the brief period of time that it took our armed forces to win the war, it was still cold in America when it ended. But my personal war with the postal inspectors heated up again in March. My lawyer contacted me and scheduled a court appearance with the postal inspectors in May at the United States General District Court in Roanoke. I got some publicity over a *reverse discrimination* case. One particular radio station in Roanoke called me and asked "What insane asylum did you escape from?" How dare I fight for my rights as an honorably discharged veteran. I wonder what asylum hired the people on that particular radio station.

Needless to say, I lost the *reverse discrimination* case, but the defendants became *politically correct* in the court room. The United States Postal Inspection Service knew that I wasn't Hispanic, as my last name was Harrison. Well, what if my mother was Hispanic? But the postal inspector recruiter gave testimony that I was the better candidate after everything was said and done. Although the US Postal Service won this particular case of *reverse discrimination*, the federal judge chided the postal inspector recruiters about their negligence in this particular case. The judge stated "Though this man failed to prove his *reverse discrimination* case, he had grounds for negligence on your part." I didn't appeal the ruling, still smarting over the large amount of money that I had spent for a lawyer during three years of fighting the system.

The clique and local postal management did not let me forget my valiant, but *politically incorrect* court appearance in Roanoke. When I called the post office to request sick leave a month after the court case ended, local management typed a letter of warning for enclosure in my personnel file, about *failure to maintain a proper work schedule.* But I made an agreement with the supervisor to remove the letter of warning from my file, provided that I regularly attended work for the next six months without using any sick leave. My supervisor removed the letter from my file one night and I called the main post office requesting sick leave the next night. And people wonder why some of us *go postal.*

The summer of 1991 was quiet except for brother Robert remarrying his fiance, Icie. Meanwhile Andy's new wife Jennifer gave birth to a son in July, and his parents named him Joshua. Faye loved her new grandson very much and spent a lot of quality time with him during the next couple of years. In fact Faye and I spent a lot of great quality time together in our country castle. It was my only respite from the US Postal Service. In fact the main post office in Roanoke had very different ideas about my career, than me on the same subject.

The clique and their friends in management did everything possible to limit my upward mobility in the postal service. Some of these people even informed me, that because I filed two different EEO complaints, I would never get promoted out of the mail handler craft. Unfortunately these rumor carriers turned out to be right. During my remaining career, I signed the overtime desired list in the winter to get extra money while the mail volume was high, and then worked eight hour shifts or took vacation time while the weather was warm and the mail volume was down. Meanwhile Faye worked with Andy's ex-girlfriend, making extra money at carnivals. Faye assembled fruit cups and strawberry short cakes, while Andy's former girlfriend worked on the grill. In May 1992 while working at the Memorial Day carnival in Roanoke, known as *Festival in the Park*, Faye contacted pneumonia and nearly died then. In fact had I not transported her to the doctor that day, she would have died. With the pneumonia ordeal lasting about a week, I definitely went into *low profile* status while at work.

As Christmas approached in the year 1992, I heard some bad news about sister Janet. I had heard that her marriage had ended due to irreconcilable differences. Soon she found someone whom she had always liked and their relationship blossomed. A few months later, I met her new beau and realized that Janet had made the right choice about her life. As of this writing, Janet still has the same man in her life, except that he has been her husband for many years. After this discovery I took a chance at work and the gamble paid off for me.

The United States Postal Service had a *buyout* in 1992 and some of the employees actually took the money and left the service. One of these particular employees that took the *buyout*, had an afternoon shift job with Sundays and Mondays off from work. When management posted this job in December, I bid on it and became the successful bidder due to union rules of seniority. I started my new position during the first week of January 1993 and got some night sleep for the first time in over nine years with one weekend day off from work.

I felt like a new man and stayed awake for 11 A.M. church services. Soon Faye and I joined the local Lutheran church in Blue Ridge known as Glade Creek Lutheran Church. I finally felt like a Christian again after spending nearly ten years on the night shift. Faye cooked and sang in the choir at the Lutheran church, in addition to her duties at the carnivals on occasions like *Festival in the Park*. Faye had become a *reborn Christian* and was happier than ever. We attended the candlelight service at the local Lutheran church in 1993 and with the snow accumulation earlier that week, experienced a true *White Christmas*. It was another of those wonderful experiences that one loves to remember forever.

As the year 1994 began, I signed the overtime desired list for mail handlers, working twelve hour shifts daily. I wanted to pay the second mortgage so we could refinance our country home at a much lower interest rate. Our existing home loan was at a high interest rate and twenty-three years of payments remained on our home. By refinancing this loan, we obtained a lower interest rate and a fifteen year mortgage. By completing this transaction, I only had to pay a few dollars more in monthly payments. Faye and I were completely satisfied with this development when we signed the new loan papers in March and I removed my name from the overtime desired list. This meant that when I retired from the US Postal Service in the year 2009, that we would own our country home. The afternoon shift also agreed with my body better as I was getting better sleep quality and was generally in a better mood. But Faye was also in the mood to do something as well.

That summer my wife spent a week in Baltimore with her three daughters there. I drove her there one weekend and brought her home on the following weekend. In retrospect I am always glad that I did that in 1994. Faye's daughters always felt that I had taken their mother from them, although we had constantly invited them to visit us in Virginia. This may sound a bit selfish, but Faye was a country girl at heart and loved the mountains. She was perfectly content at home observing the majestic mountains at a distance and watching the surging stream up close and personal.

With the summer of 1994 upon us, several issues dominated the scene in my family. My mother and father sold their beach front house at the Outer Banks and moved to Thaxton, Virginia. Dad loved to fish but mom tired of the large number of storms that curtailed their electric usage in North Carolina. Also dad had back surgery during the previous year and was not the fisherman of yore. My parents then bought a refurnished mobile home with an adjoining two car garage. As my parents had two sons close in proximity, they had someone to assist them in their elderly needs now. Meanwhile my brother Michael found a new girlfriend named Brenda, whom he married in March 1995. I didn't know about the wedding until it was over, but by then I had my own major issues.

In December, I noticed a protrusion on Faye's forehead and recommended that she see a doctor soon. As the protrusion disappeared the following week, we forgot about it and enjoyed the Christmas holidays as usual. My wife had been losing a few pounds weekly, and was having small bloody discharges monthly. Faye joked about it and said "My menstrual cycle has returned after a ten year absence." But in the end the joke was on both of us. When the protrusion reappeared on Faye's forehead in January, she finally decided to see a doctor about it. The protrusion that we saw turned out to be a tumor, which was a sign of cancer of the uterus. My wife of twelve years was terminally ill.

At first the cancer didn't seem too terrible, so we had our wills notarized while my wife was still cognizant of her surroundings. Actually her mind remained sound for months while her body deteriorated from the cancer. Faye's daughters visited her for a week in May and my sister and her fiance visited as well. The one person who performed the best during this time of crisis was Faye's son, Andy. He was the unsung hero of the hour for his mother. Andy and hospice, which administered medical treatment to terminally ill patients, were a constant in Faye's daily life until her death. As was typical of Faye's character, she made a joke at my expense before her death saying "It's your fault Harrison for marrying such an old bag."

One week later, Faye slipped into a coma and did not emerge from it until June 30th. While Faye was in the coma, the union at work had negotiated with management, for me to be on emergency leave for the duration of my wife's fatal illness. Under the new family leave law, local management complied with my request. When Faye opened her eyes after emerging from the coma, she looked up and told me that she loved me. That same day the Lutheran pastor visited our home and said "She looks at peace with the world." Her doctor and hospice nurse visited Faye that same day and made the same observation.

The next day on July 1, 1995, at 4:45 A.M., Lavonia Faye Harrison passed away. I notified hospice and every family member of her death. Visitation was that Sunday at Oakey's Funeral Home with burial that Monday at Old Dominion Memorial Gardens. I remained strong until the Lutheran pastor read Psalm 23 at the burial site and I lost it, sobbing uncontrollably for my deceased wife. After burying the best person that I have ever known, I wanted to die as well. But my mother stopped me and said "You're not dead. You're still young enough to go on living and you will." That message helped me but the next event helped me in a greater way, and restored my religious faith as well.

Faye had promised me during those months of sickness that she would give me a sign when she ascended into heaven. Janet, her fiancé, and I had fallen asleep at my home after the funeral. My sister and I awakened from our sleep and we decided to go to the cemetery at that instant. When we arrived there, I noticed all of the flowers, but also saw a balloon tied to a child's grave, next to Faye's grave. The balloon was given to Faye as a memento by a three year old girl, whom Faye had babysat. As I tried to untie the balloon, it suddenly jumped out of my hands and veered straight toward the sun as if being pulled by God. Although most balloons tend to sway in the breeze, this one moved in a perfectly straight line. Faye's favorite song was *I'll Fly Away* and this song was played at her funeral. Looking straight into the heavens, my sister Janet yelled "I'll fly away". If this wasn't a true sign of redemption, then I do not know the definition of the word sign. Janet and I embraced each other, reassured that Faye had found a place in heaven. Meanwhile I wouldn't find any peace for a long period of time. Actually I found just the opposite during the next several years of my life.

Chapter VIII

"ROAD RAGE" IN ROANOKE VIRGINIA

The day after Faye's funeral, mom called and asked me to come to her house for a Fourth of July celebration. I said no thanks, but thanked her for being there for me during my time of sorrow. That day I decided to go to Andy's house and enjoyed the fireworks with Andy and his four year old son Joshua. Andy was a good cook like his mother, so we ate well. Just like his mother, he made me laugh that day. He said "I'm glad that we didn't have to bury mom today. She hated the heat." He grinned as he said that. He was right about the weather as the mercury rose to 95 degrees that day. The previous day's high was 78 degrees, which was cool by July standards. It was the last time that laughed for a long time.

I just felt numb for a while, even when I returned to work on July 10th. My co-workers had given me three hundred dollars and two sympathy cards in behalf of my wife's death. I was astounded that I had that many friends at the main post office. These people were not clique members. As work progressed in July, I remembered something that Faye had told me prior to her death. She said that I had not met my *soul mate* yet and after she died, she wanted me to look for her. I told Faye that she was my *soul mate*, but she insisted that I was wrong because of our twenty year age difference. In pursuit of a *soul mate*, I began dating six weeks after my wife's death.

The first lady that I dated, was an old friend from Kroger's Store who was nice to me during my ordeal. During our first date all I did was talk about Faye, and so I was shocked when this lady asked me to see her again. The relationship got semi-serious by November, but ended the week before Christmas. By this time, the Roanoke area received its first snowfall of the season on November 11th. That date was Faye's first birthday in heaven and the significance of that event was not lost on my sister. Janet called me that day and informed me that Baltimore experienced its first recorded snowfall of the year. Now Janet and I were both aware that Faye Harrison was resting in heaven.

On Christmas day, I drove to my parents' house in Thaxton for a somber Christmas dinner. My first serious relationship after Faye's death had ended recently and I was alone at Christmas for the first time in many years. I even contemplated suicide, but I did not have the nerve to pull the trigger. I just wanted the holidays to hurry and end so I could return to work.

I had bought a 1994 Pontiac Sunbird during the previous year and decided to pay the remaining balance owed on the vehicle by working overtime during the dreadful winter of 1996, which had massive snowfalls. I signed my name to the overtime desired list and worked twelve hour shifts on a daily basis. At least there was a reasonable goal at this time. By the middle of March, I paid off the balance owed on the vehicle and withdrew my name from the overtime desired list. I owned a vehicle with few miles on the odometer and began dating again. The weather did not cooperate that year and every weekend from mid-March until the first weekend of April, there was snow or a threat of snow. In retrospect I think someone in heaven was trying to prevent me from getting hurt. In Faye's last month of life, she read my palm and described the kind of future to expect in life. In complete candor Faye said that "You will encounter the greatest obstacle of your life in the next few years and after you pass that nearly fatal test, you will lead a long and fulfilling life." Faye was uncanny at predicting the future and I am living proof of her accuracy.

During the second weekend of April I met a short, rotund, blue-eyed blonde through a dating service. We made love after our first date in my home and one month later we got engaged. At a Memorial Day cookout at my home, two of my fiance's sons tried to dissuade from marrying their mother. They warned me and said that I would be sorry. For the record, my fiance's oldest son was thirty and the other son was in his late 20s. My fiance was middle-aged like me. By now after losing one true love, I just wanted to love someone who would say yes to me. I was lonely then and still in mourning. An older Lutheran lady at church warned me during that spring, saying "There are things worse in life than being alone." I soon discovered that the Lutheran lady was right.

I continued dating my fiance all summer and discovered that we had some serious issues. I began to get an idea of what to expect, but I chose to ignore the obvious signs. My country home experienced major changes to its interior that summer. I had to paint every interior room and remove all of the existing carpet before my new wife would move into my home. There had to be no evidence of my deceased wife's presence. Furthermore my fiancé spent a large amount of my money on a new bedroom suite, and sold my eleven year old bedroom furniture for little money as it reminded her of the past. I guess it was difficult to move into the home of someone, whose wife had perished in the very same building. Matters deteriorated on the eve of our wedding.

During that day my fiancé had an automobile accident, smashing the front end of her car into the rear bumper of a busload of children, who were headed for a Christian child care center. Fortunately no one was hurt in the collision and the bus was not damaged. The only damage was to my fiance's 1990 Pontiac Grand Am. The vehicle sustained a considerable amount of damage to the bumper, hood, and fenders. The police officer at the scene of the accident did not give her a ticket, as she was getting married the next day. The following day MasterCard called me an hour before the wedding, and informed me that I had exceeded the spending limit of that particular credit card. Always having A-1 credit prior to the year 1996, my credit rating plummeted quickly that year.

We got married on August 24th and the ill-fated marriage deteriorated daily. We traveled to Ocean City, Maryland for our honeymoon and had a tenth floor ocean side suite for the occasion. My new wife constantly complained about not having an ocean front room for the honeymoon. During those six days, she had her hair dyed, cut, set, and then re-dyed again. The total cost of all this hair nonsense was unbelievable. Even the honeymoon was blasé itself. When we prepared to leave that following Saturday, I noticed the stormy waves striking the shore line. I believed that this weather was a premonition of my future.

We returned home to Blue Ridge and I actually looked forward to returning to work. I signed the overtime desired list and attempted to get all of the overtime to pay for these massive new expenses. With a successful job bid that summer, I had weekends off but still worked second shift. At this moment I just needed money for all of my newly discovered issues.

As Christmas 1996 approached, my wife wanted to buy a lot of presents for her large family for the joyous occasion. I told her that I didn't have the money, but she used my credit card and I allowed her to do this, making my financial burden even greater. By now I had three major credit cards over the limit in four months of marriage with no end in sight. Even making a good salary with overtime earnings, I was pinned to the mat. If I said no to my wife, I did not trust or love her. On my wife's birthday, I bought her a newer Pontiac Grand Am, which added to my financial woes. Her old model had some serious issues with all of the previous damage done to it. I either had to spend a lot of money to restore it or trade the car for a newer model. I preferred the latter course of action, although it cost me even more money, and contributed to my financial demise.

In March 1997, I applied for one last credit card. In two days my wife exceeded the credit card limit, buying a large amount of clothes for her wardrobe. I was in a state of shock after discovering about the newly incurred debt. We were deep in debt and things got worse. Again I contributed to my own demise by allowing matters to deteriorate.

On March 8, 1997, the *road rage* incident occurred. The *Roanoke Times* went to great lengths describing the circumstances of that day without interviewing a single credible witness. The newspaper tried to coerce me into telling my side of the story during that time but I refused, citing lawyer confidentiality. My wife became hysterical during this ordeal with the other driver's dangerous ways. The other driver was a psychiatric patient as he stated under oath at the trial, so I remain the only credible witness concerning the incident in question. Throughout this entire autobiography I have presented the facts as I remember them, and my recollection of this incident is the same. I can honestly say that I have never pretended to be innocent about this incident. What one needs to decide is whether the other driver was a victim of *road rage* or another guilty party involved in the incident.

While driving my wife to work at Roanoke Memorial Hospital that Saturday, we took Williamson Road southbound over the viaduct through the Campbell Avenue intersection. Then a large 1971 Chevrolet pickup truck *tailgated* my small Pontiac Sunbird, necessitating a lane change into the right lane. Stopping for the Church Avenue red light, I glared at the pickup truck's driver but his eyes were focused ahead. Then both vehicles proceeded southbound through the Franklin Road intersection at about thirty-five miles per hour in a thirty mile per hour speed limit zone. As I proceeded in the right lane up the hill to the Elm Avenue intersection, I heard the roar of an engine and the same pickup truck sped past my vehicle and nearly struck us, while swerving into the right lane. My wife was screaming at the top of her lungs "He's trying to kill us." I saw *The Intimidator* on the truck's license plate frame and determined to confront this particular individual.

As the Elm Avenue traffic light turned green, *The Intimidator* drove past the light, swerved to the right, and screeched to a stop, prior to entering Roanoke Community Hospital's parking garage. I stopped my vehicle behind the pickup truck and the driver emerged from the vehicle and verbally confronted me. I exited my vehicle and yelled at the other driver "What the hell is the matter with you? Are you trying to kill us?" The other driver then yelled back "I'll do as I damn well please. Watch me." I waited for what seemed like a lifetime, but was probably one minute for him to drive his vehicle into the parking garage. This white male driver never put the truck in gear and chose to confront me instead of driving his pickup truck into the garage.

At this point in the *road rage* situation, I counted two times that an altercation could have been avoided. By this time I was worried about being stabbed again, so I grabbed a tire iron out of the trunk and brought it for self defense. When I peered through the driver's door, I saw the other driver trying to retrieve something out of the glove compartment with his right hand. I knew from previous experience, that I did not want to discover what that could be. As I opened the driver's side door, he swung his right hand at me from the glove compartment and I blocked it. Fearing for my life, I held the tire iron in my right hand with the lug wrench part in my fist and the prying edge near my right elbow. I then proceeded to grab him in a headlock and extracted his body from the front seat. I then flipped his body over my shoulder and down to the concrete at the entrance of the parking garage.

During this entire ordeal I concentrated on his right hand, to see if he had a weapon in it. When his body hit the pavement, the hand was empty and I unconsciously dropped the tire iron. This produced a loud clang which the hospital security guard heard at that time. Then I lost my temper and kicked the other driver in the ribs. My wife screamed at me to stop and I complied with her demand. By now she had calmed down and I needed to do so too. Then the shirtless security guard arrived with his pistol and shield. If this case had gone to a jury, the security guard would have testified to the noise of a tire iron clang, as well as my kicking of the other driver's ribs. When the other driver sat up, I saw blood behind his ear and initially failed to comprehend how he received this cut. Because the other driver had a two stitch cut about an inch long, the state of Virginia charged me with malicious wounding, which was a felony, and carried a prison sentence of two to four years duration.

The rest of that weekend after this incident, I deduced how the other driver received his two stitch cut. When I pulled him out of the front seat, the prying part of the tire iron dug into his skin and created the base of the cut, while I provided the friction with a tight headlock and subsequent flip of the other driver to the concrete. That was the only possible explanation for a cut that was one inch long and required two stitches to close it.

On Monday after I worked the afternoon shift, I reported to the Botetourt County Magistrate's Office. I even brought the tire iron, though the magistrate said that he did not need it. I went about business as usual until May, when I received a contract from a buyer for my country home. Even though I sold my house, I hated to leave it. In desperate financial straits, I netted several thousand dollars from the sale of my home and rented a two bedroom townhouse in Roanoke County for my estranged wife. In June we separated and I temporarily moved to my ex-stepson Andy's residence.

I then hired a great lawyer and withheld a few thousand dollars from the proceeds of the sale of the house for my impending trial. While separated from my wife, I made the wisest decision of the year and filed chapter 13 bankruptcy. At a pre-trial hearing that month, my lawyer and I met the victim of *road rage*. Even though he was fifty-nine years old and I was forty-five then, the other driver looked much older, with his withered skin and frail features. The other driver at the pre-trial hearing claimed that in addition to the cut behind his ear, that he spent thirty days in a sanitarium and had sore ribs. He also claimed that I broke the lock on the driver's door of his truck and it required one hundred and five dollars to repair it. Later my lawyer requested me to take this case before a judge and not a jury. My lawyer also requested that I plead *no contest* before a judge, as I was guilty of certain actions during this incident. I took my lawyer's advice and prepared for the worst.

The biggest mistake that I made in June was returning to my estranged wife. She agreed in principle to my conditions about improving our marriage. After a week of improvement, our marriage retreated into the same old routine with irreconcilable differences between us. But the good news for me was that there were no more credit cards to be used or abused. But she was miserable and I became that way as well. I tried one more move and that was to sell my 1994 Pontiac Sunbird back to the dealership. I would then buy a private owner's 1988 Mercury Topaz. I hoped that the money made while exchanging vehicles would make our life easier that summer, but it only had a temporary effect. In a few weeks the money was gone and both of us became miserable again. Meanwhile I successfully bid on a daylight job at the main post office.

In September, I started working at my new job from 7:30 A.M. until 3:30 P.M. with Friday and Saturday as nonscheduled days. Actually due to my wife's insistence, I bid for that job to spend more quality time at home. Unfortunately some of the clique members became my co-workers and I wasn't very pleased with that development. Nevertheless I kept quiet about my *road rage* incident while at work and my lawyer continued to lobby for continuances in my behalf throughout the year. In November the tea pot boiled over and I got scalded.

On November 7th I was arraigned before a judge, commonwealth's attorney, my lawyer, the other driver and a solitary witness. The witness was a *Roanoke Times* crime reporter and the next day the *road rage* incident became page one news in the *Virginia section* of the *Roanoke Times*. I was appalled at the disturbing rhetoric of the article in the newspaper, but my mother was devastated. One of the reasons that I wrote this autobiography was to write the truth about this incident, unlike the diatribe that the *Roanoke Times* published, that upset my mother so badly.

The *Roanoke Times* reporter stated that a postal employee forcefully assaulted a senior citizen for no apparent reason, yanking him out of his vehicle and nearly beating him to death. This reporter further implied that the tire iron played a key role in this assault. By this time I had become acquainted with the local brand of *yellow journalism* or the distortion of facts in order to sell a newspaper. That Friday I worked a half day as it was my nonscheduled day and everyone at the post office was talking about this article. On Sunday I worked at the post office without incident.

When I reported to work on Monday, I was led out of the building to my car, after extracting all of my personal effects. In my opinion I had been convicted of a crime before I ever went on trial. I was placed on administrative leave by the postal service for the next month, requiring a daily telephone call to the post office in order to receive a paycheck. Of course the direction that this thirty day administrative leave headed, was for my job termination in December. While all of this action took place, my life took another downward spiral in late November of 1997.

My wife and I had a very contentious relationship and it ended the night of Thanksgiving. We had agreed to spend half of the day with her family and the rest of the day with my family in Franklin County. Sister Janet had driven from Baltimore and looked forward to being with me. I wanted to see them but did so alone. When I returned that night my wife was agitated and we became involved in a push and shove incident. I was tired of everything and pushed her forcefully to the carpet, fracturing a bone behind her knee. I left the scene and drove to Franklin County. But she called her daughter who called 911, which was the right course of action. With the recently passed domestic violence laws in Virginia then, the police arrived first on the scene and looked for me. Eventually the ambulance arrived and took care of my wife's needs.

That same night I changed my mind about driving to Franklin County and telephoned my wife to check on her condition. The police intervened and asked if they could meet me to discuss the matter. When I met them, they handcuffed me and escorted me to Roanoke County jail. Now that I was in jail, I realized what a terrible thing that I had done to my wife and wished her a speedy recovery. Despite our issues, I never intentionally tried to injure her. I remained in jail for four days, when I appeared before a judge for arraignment. As an old vehicle was my only property, the judge determined to keep me in jail despite the absence of a criminal record. At the last minute my *road rage* lawyer appeared in the court room and immediately met with my parents, who were there. As a result of arraignment and no bail, I cried in the cell and wondered how my life had deteriorated. I had lost my job, injured my wife, sold my house and lost everything. I begged God for forgiveness in the solitude of a jail cell. At a time in my life when I was pinned by the devil, God quickly responded to my request.

I telephoned my mother that night from jail and she gave me great news. My *road rage* lawyer had met with the commonwealth's attorney concerning the domestic violence charge. The two lawyers agreed to a surety bond on my parents' house in return for my release from jail. The following morning I was released from jail and immediately went to my wife's townhouse and withdrew my effects for transportation to my parents' home. I even notified the local police to insure that the transportation of my effects was done in a smooth manner. The marriage was over and should have never taken place, due to the difference in our personalities. I made this decision then and bear equal responsibility for what went wrong in this relationship.

I lived with my parents during most of the next six months while my legal affairs were settled. My mother said "If you return to your estranged wife, I will disown you." Mom certainly didn't have to tell me twice. The following week the postal service terminated me, but I started another job as a pickup truck driver for a windshield delivery company. I delivered windshields and their accessories to all parts of southwest Virginia. This job enabled me to continue my monthly payments for chapter 13 bankruptcy. In January 1998, I had two different court dates. On January 15th I was to stand trial for the *road rage* incident. The actual charges were malicious wounding which was a felony, and tampering with a vehicle which was a misdemeanor. With dad taking out an additional mortgage, we offered the *road rage* victim ten thousand dollars to settle everything. He refused this generous offer but my lawyer got a continuance until March 2, 1998.

During the following week I confronted my estranged wife in Juvenile and Domestic Relations Court. The judge convicted me of assault and battery and scheduled me to spend the next six months in jail with no contact with my estranged wife during this time. I was devastated by the length of this misdemeanor sentence and sat in absolute shock in my holding cell. The following morning the deputies awakened me for breakfast, and I told them that I wished to starve to death. They were shocked at this development as I only had ten days left to serve in jail. I was visibly relieved and asked how that was possible. They told me that five of the six months of that sentence were vacated and that I only needed to serve one month. As assault and battery was a misdemeanor, I only had to serve half of that thirty day sentence. As I had previously served four days in December, I only had ten more days of jail time left. By now I reconsidered my options about breakfast.

After leaving Roanoke County Jail the end of January, I returned to my parents' home in Thaxton. I thanked both of my parents for all that they had done, and told them that I would attempt to repay them for everything. I had a renewed sense of purpose at the age of forty-six in February 1998. I returned to my job of transporting windshields and paid the chapter 13 payments for February and March. I was still breathing but had one more major obstacle.

During the last week of February, the *road rage* victim obtained an attorney who was a friend of my lawyer. At the *eleventh hour* of my trial on March 2nd, the two lawyers made an agreement. I paid the other driver ten thousand dollars before the inception of the trial and then paid him an additional five thousand dollars more within a year of this trial. The other driver then signed a legal document entitled a *Satisfaction and Accord* and received a ten thousand dollar check. By signing that legal document, the other driver could never summon me to civil court and sue me for future damages for any injuries that he sustained in this matter. After I paid that additional amount, he was out of my life forever. But there was still a *road rage* trial at hand.

The judge was a very fair man and listened to everything that was said about me. I had five witnesses in my behalf, four from work and the hospice nurse that attended to Faye's needs during her terminal illness. One postal supervisor even told the judge that if I was convicted of a misdemeanor only, that he could guarantee my retention in the postal workforce. The judge reduced the malicious wounding charge to a misdemeanor conviction of assault and battery. The judge gave me three months of jail time and as it was a misdemeanor, I was only required to serve one and a half months in jail. He also found me guilty of the misdemeanor charge of tampering with a vehicle. I served one year of probation for that conviction. Together I received two years of probation. The judge then told me in no uncertain terms "You are going to get a taste of jail and how your life could be. But I want you to return to work and pay this man." I thanked him for his judgment and he gave me two weeks to get my affairs in order and report to jail.

I continued my job of delivering windshields and also continued to attend *anger management* class, which I had voluntarily done since February on legal advice from my attorney. During the second week of March, the *anger management* counselor was on leave and did not return until the first day of my incarceration. As this counseling was a prerequisite of my sentence, I sent several messages to the counselor to contact the jail authorities. Actually he did contact them on that day. Meanwhile Mail Handlers' Union Local 305 had obtained a *work release* agreement for me from high ranking postal authorities in management and labor in the city of Philadelphia. On March 17th,, local Roanoke management visited me in my cell and informed me that I was terminated from my job again. Again I was devastated and cried in my holding cell. Later the jail sergeant summoned me and told me that he wanted me to be a trustee in his jail. The sergeant told me about all of the past problems that he had personally experienced with local postal management and had grave doubts about work release for any of its employees. He further informed me that after one month as a trustee, that I would be released from his jail and free to take care of business. In the meantime there was work to be done in that jail.

On April 16, 1998, I was released from jail and never returned again. My union had filed a subsequent grievance in my behalf and on April 23rd I returned to work in my original job from the previous year. April 23rd was the date of my marriage to Faye in 1983. It was a great harbinger of things to come. The days of darkness had ended.

CHAPTER IX

EPILOGUE

When I returned to work that Thursday, I discovered quickly from certain sources that local management had circulated a petition against me saying "That Chris is a dangerous employee and prone to fits of violent temper." Roanoke postal management claimed that it was Charleston West Virginia's idea as their managers were Roanoke's superiors in the Eastern Region. My union, which was Local 305 Mail Handlers', termed it a *character assassination* of an employee, who had twelve years of work experience at the Roanoke facility without incident. The petition bombed badly as only ten signed it of the one hundred mail handlers in the Roanoke post office.

Meanwhile as I had been on the overtime desired list when I previously worked at the main post office, I remained on that list. I had many bills to pay and a short time to pay them. On my first day, I worked twelve hours and continued that trend for a long period of time. The following week my estranged wife sent me a declaration of divorce via sheriff's deputy to my parents' home in Thaxton. Mom was upset about the circumstances involved in the process, but dad was happy about this development. Dad said that she would have to prove her grounds for divorce and that I didn't have anything to worry about. After my first two full checks, I retained a female divorce lawyer of diminutive height, but a powerful resume. In the meantime I moved away from my parents' home and into a one bedroom apartment, just four miles from work. It was the perfect residence for me at this time.

At our first separation hearing in June, my lawyer and I met my estranged wife and her lawyer. The only issue that required a decision with regard to property was our two automobiles. I was driving an old car and she was driving a newer car at the time. During my first six weeks of work, I had spent several hundred dollars to maintain the old jalopy. My estranged wife had a fairly new vehicle with monthly payments over five years duration. Although I had religiously made the first twelve payments toward ownership of that vehicle, I had no idea whether my estranged wife had made any further payments. Of course my ignorance of details was due to the fact that I was convicted of *domestic violence* and was to have no contact with my estranged wife for the duration of the sentence.

With her daughter and both lawyers present, my estranged wife asked for a large amount of money for alimony payments from the female judge so that she could continue making automobile payments. The judge granted her less alimony per month than she requested until finalization of our divorce. As my estranged wife had only made two monthly payments on the car in five months, it was repossessed by the bank during the following week. As I was the principal wage earner for the car loan, the bank called me for the outstanding balance owed on the car. I informed them that I had filed chapter 13 bankruptcy and as this vehicle was included in the original plan, the bank needed to contact my bankruptcy lawyer. I never heard from this collector again.

By the last week of June 1998, I received an extra check from the US Postal Service for thirty-two days of pay. As the Roanoke post office management had disobeyed their superiors' orders, and fired me after having a *work release* agreement, they were obligated to pay me for the entire time that I would have worked at that pursuit. Our Mail Handlers' Union Local Chapter 305 came through again for me. The mail handlers' union had a fine administrative vice president and the best chief shop steward in the nation. They saved my job and I owe both of them a huge measure of gratitude. The very next day I paid back the I.R.S. for failure to pay enough federal income tax from the previous year. In this case the US Postal Service paid off an existing debt to the Internal Revenue Service. What a novel concept with one branch of the federal government paying another branch of the federal government for incurred debts.

As the year 1998 progressed, I continued to pay all of my debts. In August I finished attendance at my *anger management* counseling and its weekly fee. My next goal was divorce but I would not reach that objective until January 1999. In the meantime, I attended Trinity Lutheran Church weekly and thanked God for his help in this matter. By the end of the year 1998, I had grossed a lot of money in nine months work.

On January 4, 1999, I ended a miserable fifteen month marriage. My ex-wife wanted a large amount of alimony for the rest of her life or until remarried on the grounds of physical abuse and desertion. My female lawyer embarrassed my ex-wife in front of the nationally renowned judge. The judge only awarded her half of the monthly alimony payments that she wanted for one year. Additionally the female judge dismissed the grounds for divorce against me. I then tripled the alimony payments and paid the balance to my ex-wife by June 1999. She was now out of my life forever.

During the same time, I had been paying the *road rage* victim a small amount of money per month for the last four months of 1998. But I still owed him a large sum of money and that sum had to be paid in its entirety by March 1999. In late February I paid the remaining balance owed and danced on his attorney's steps in downtown Roanoke. Now he was out of my life forever as well.

During all of 1999, I continued working overtime, lived in my apartment, and reported to my probation officer on a monthly basis. And of course I continued to attend Trinity Lutheran Church on Sundays and prayed for God's assistance. The beat went on that year for me. By August I paid my dad the rest of the money that I had borrowed from him. He said that it was the greatest thing that I had ever done in my life and that he was finally proud of me. I was just glad that dad lived in Virginia when I needed him most.

In December 1999 I finished paying for my chapter 13 bankruptcy. I had paid about 40% of the personal debt that I had incurred by June 1997. By paying 40% of my total debt without interest, I rebuilt my finances, without waiting the required seven years under Chapter 7 bankruptcy to begin anew. I chose to finish my chapter 13 payments early so that I wouldn't have to fear the arrival of the year 2000. I entered the new millennium without any secured or unsecured debt. I did not owe any money to anyone except for the monthly rent for a one bedroom apartment. I looked at the December calendar and realized that it was Christmas Eve. For the first time in years I was happy again. I knew that the mourning period for my wife's death was finally over after four agonizing years. I had grossed more money in 1999 than in 1998 and paid all of my outstanding debts. I was just glad to be single and heading into the new millennium.

I continued working overtime in the year 2000 and saved several thousand dollars in three months for the purchase of another home. At the end of March I finished my two year probationary period and was free to do whatever I chose to do with my life. In May I bought a cheaply priced house in northeast Roanoke and moved in by Memorial Day. While walking through the living room, I was startled to see the image of my deceased wife. I saw her clearly in one of her old housewife outfits. At this moment I knew that she was pleased with my progress. I was pleased as well and with God's help, I had escaped from all debt. I even ventured to Archbishop Curley High School for my 30th high school reunion in June, thoroughly enjoying the drive to Baltimore. It felt great to be free of all ties to everything at that time.

The following month I purchased a 1999 Toyota Corolla after my car was *rear ended* in an automobile accident. I was physically unharmed but the old jalopy was totaled. I now owned a credit card and became busy reestablishing my credit. Being *level headed* now, I returned to dating. But I was in no hurry to ever reach the altar again. I dated a lot during this period of time but found no one of substance. On November 11, 2003, I met a ravishing, blue-eyed redhead through a mutual friend. My life changed again but this time for the better.

Lena Lytton Harrison became my new wife in March 2005. An astute businesswoman, she had similar interests to me. She loved sports, reading and gardening. Most importantly she had lost her first husband of twenty-three years to cancer, and knew what it was like to lose a loved one. Our marriage has continued to flourish and each year brings better things. During my last year in the United States Postal Service, I passed both the Virginia Communication and Literacy Assessment and the Social Studies Aptitude Examination to obtain a five year certification in the state of Virginia for teaching history and social studies.

On October 31, 2009, I received a *buyout* from the US Postal Service, with ten thousand dollars immediately and five thousand dollars exactly one year after retirement in addition to my monthly civil service retirement checks. This *buyout* is very similar to a *road rage* agreement that I made in March 1998. It just proved the old adage about what comes around, goes around. At the close of this chapter in my life, I thank God for all of the great friends that He has placed in my life, allowing me to attain what I have today. However I have one final bit of advice.

When driving your vehicle, never lose control of your emotions. If another motorist confronts you, use your cell phone to call the proper authorities. Never take the law into your own hands as I once did. Whatever you do, never allow a stranger to ruin you life. I wish to thank those who may read my autobiography and I hope that you have some new insight about *road rage* through my humbling experiences. May God bless all of you, as He has blessed me.